T0114110

Cambridge Elements ≡

Elements in Politics and Society in Latin America
edited by
Maria Victoria Murillo
Columbia University
Tulia G. Falleti
University of Pennsylvania
Juan Pablo Luna
The Pontifical Catholic University of Chile
Andrew Schrank
Brown University

BEYOND 'PLATA O PLOMO'

Drugs and State Reconfiguration in Colombia

Gustavo Duncan
EAFIT University

Shaftesbury Road, Cambridge CB2 8EA, United Kingdom

One Liberty Plaza, 20th Floor, New York, NY 10006, USA

477 Williamstown Road, Port Melbourne, VIC 3207, Australia

314–321, 3rd Floor, Plot 3, Splendor Forum, Jasola District Centre, New Delhi – 110025, India

103 Penang Road, #05–06/07, Visioncrest Commercial, Singapore 238467

Cambridge University Press is part of Cambridge University Press & Assessment, a department of the University of Cambridge.

We share the University's mission to contribute to society through the pursuit of education, learning and research at the highest international levels of excellence.

www.cambridge.org
Information on this title: www.cambridge.org/9781108810326

DOI: 10.1017/9781108893909

First published 2022

A catalogue record for this publication is available from the British Library.

ISBN 978-1-108-81032-6 Paperback
ISSN 2515-5253 (online)
ISSN 2515-5245 (print)

Beyond 'plata o plomo'

Drugs and State Reconfiguration in Colombia

Elements in Politics and Society in Latin America

DOI: 10.1017/9781108893909
First published online: August 2022

Gustavo Duncan
EAFIT University

Author for correspondence: Gustavo Duncan, gustavoduncan@yahoo.com

Abstract: This Element introduces the concept of oligopoly of coercion (i.e. a situation in which the state and private armies simultaneously have overlapping control of the means of coercion necessary to rule society) to interpret the interaction between drug trafficking and reconfiguration of the state in Colombia. Three factors are central to this interpretation: Corruption in oligopolies of coercion must be understood as a payment by drug traffickers for acting like a parallel state; there is a clear association between the location of the oligopolies of coercion and the geography of the state; the politics of drug trafficking in Colombia should be understood in the context of the ways in which peripheral societies access global markets through the ruling institutions of private armies. With these factors in mind, the author focuses on the dynamics of the reconfiguration of the state in Colombia after the cocaine boom of the mid-1970s.

Keywords: criminal governance, sociology of the state, drug trafficking, organized crime, corruption

ISBNs: 9781108810326 (PB), 9781108893909 (OC)
ISSNs: 2515-5253 (online), 2515-5245 (print)

Contents

1 Introduction

The guerrilla was not the only problem ... before the paramilitaries, if someone stole livestock or a neighbor's land, nothing happened. There was no state ... when the paramilitaries arrived, those things ended. The one who stole paid dearly. Look, they subpoenaed the mayors of these towns to account for the expenditures of the public budget ... before the paramilitaries, each drug trafficker produced and transported their drugs separately and denounced the others out of sheer envy. When the paramilitaries arrived, they told the drug traffickers that from now on all their drugs would be produced and transported by them. The fights between drug traffickers were over.

Notes made from memory from a conversation with a public official in Cesar (Colombia), some time in 2000.

In 2000, I was not planning to write about drug trafficking. I worked in an agency of the national government of Colombia. My role was to decide which municipalities could enter a subsidy program in education and health. In my visits to evaluate the municipalities, I observed a recurrent situation: armed civilians, some with rifles and M-60 machine guns, were monitoring the population. When I asked the locals who these people were, they dodged the subject. Then, in private, some local officials told me the armed civilians were paramilitaries. Indeed, some officials, who had gained more confidence to speak out, told me that the paramilitaries not only fought the guerrillas; they also administered justice, provided services to society, charged a tribute in return for these services, and – most surprising of all for me – organized the cocaine markets in the form of a regional monopoly. My intuition at the time was that this was a situation in which criminals were acting like a state.

I found the matter perplexing and fascinating and since then have devoted myself to studying the matter. Over the years, I have conducted at least fifty interviews with drug traffickers, paramilitaries, and members of the armed forces with links to these groups. Some of these interviews were conducted in prisons across Colombia, others in places (cities, municipalities, and regions) where these nonstate armed groups used their formidable power and, at times, ruled unopposed. My original intuition proved to be right: Criminals were assuming the functions proper to a state. These same operatives openly recognized this. But I found it to be a much more complex reality than that of criminals ruling communities on the fringes of the state. There was a constant struggle to define the contours of criminal governance (i.e., to what extent did criminal organizations rule – was it with the blessing or connivance of the state?), an intriguing topic that has informed the emergence of a fascinating agenda (see Arias 2017; Lessing 2020). Politicians, members of the security agencies, and various public officials were mediating the matter while taking advantage of the situation to advance their interests. Tensions between the state, mediators, and criminal organizations, although usually kept under control, sometimes flared up. Some private armies aspired to extend their territorial control, or sometimes the state intervened in a region to consolidate something close to a legitimate monopoly of force. Paramilitaries, drug traffickers, and state officials recounted these episodes, each from their own perspective.

Communities were not passive. While people resented the violence and abuses perpetrated by private armies that were criminal in nature, they also found in drug surpluses a solution to the isolation of local markets. In many interviews, people spoke of the local economy as it had been before, and as it was after drug trafficking: never before had so much commerce and consumption been available in spaces so distant from the main national markets. Yet not everything was about money: Amid the interaction between the ruling institutions of drug traffickers and the state, people were trying to resolve their demands for order and protection. Beyond fear and oppression, they collaborated with private armies to prevent robberies, rapes, and injustices carried out by other members of the community. Similarly, they used the state to access other services such as education, health, and property titles.

What surprised me the most was to find that the expansion of drug trafficking was interacting with an impressive process of state reconfiguration, in which the nature of its authority throughout the territory – either in a partial or a total manner – would be permanently redefined. In this Element, I propose an interpretation of this process of interaction between drug trafficking and the reconfiguration of the state in Colombia. This interpretation can be applied to other countries that supply the world drug market and whose central authority is not in dispute. The Colombian state have never been at risk of collapsing due to drug trafficking. What has been at stake is "the monopoly on the legitimate use of physical force" (Weber 1944) in certain spaces out of the control of the central state. There, instead of a monopoly of coercion by the state, an oligopoly of coercion has existed whereby the state and private armies involved in drug trafficking simultaneously have overlapping control of the means of coercion necessary to rule society. The concept of oligopoly of coercion is best conceptualized as a continuum between areas where private armies have almost total control vis-à-vis an absent or subservient state at one extreme and areas where the state enjoys an unquestioned monopoly of force at the other.

Three factors are central to this interpretation. The first one is that the interactions between the state and drug traffickers within a context of reconfiguration of the local authority are more complex than those in a context of corruption. Like some large companies, drug traffickers pay for the authorities to enforce the laws on their behalf. Car manufacturers, for example, pay officials in order to steal intellectual property from their competitors; Internet search engine designers do so to evade antitrust laws; and drug dealers pay them to them pass their merchandise with impunity. But for some drug traffickers, payment is more a political issue than an economic one: they pay to act like a parallel state, with their own private armies, with power over a section of society. Professional politicians, policemen, and other authorities who receive their payments act as mediators between the central state institutions and the ruling institutions of the drug traffickers. They offer coexistence arrangements, both tacit and explicit, that mediate between criminals and formal institutions on the ground. Indeed, when violence breaks out, they direct the use of force by the state toward new balances of power in which, as far as possible, the resulting new order does not affect those mediators' power and wealth. Consequently, the interaction cannot be reduced to two players (criminals vs. central state), because the mediators, with their own political and economic interests, also determine the dynamics of coexistence and confrontation.

On the other hand, the fact that drug-trafficking armies do not intend to replace the central state makes them substantially different from guerrillas, who also rule in peripheral spaces (Arjona 2017) but often rely on drug trafficking to finance their insurgency. Because the guerrillas are attempting to topple and replace the central state, the possibilities of coexistence between them and the institutions of that state are significantly lower. Furthermore, the Colombian state has recurrently made agreements with private armies to combat guerrillas.

The second factor deals with the nature of those spaces where drug traffickers claim, to a greater or lesser degree, the functions proper to the state. Too many academics have highlighted that the criminalization of drugs by the state[1] has caused an increase in violence by organized crime, since the state forfeits its role as the market regulator. While relevant, this explanation misses some relevant aspects of this phenomenon. In this regard, I argue that the state criminalizes drugs as merchandise more than it does drugs as capital – the money that flows from the trade itself. As a result, there is a clear association between the location of the different phases of the business and the geography of the state in Colombia. The phase of crops and cocaine production, which involves mostly merchandise, is located in the periphery. By periphery, I understand those spaces far from the infrastructure of the state, population nuclei, and the large national markets (Shils 1974; Mann 1984). By contrast, the aspect related to money laundering tends to be located in the center, where the authority of the

---

[1] It is often the state that determines what really constitutes criminality, a point made by Andreas and Nadelmann (2013). I thank an anonymous reviewer for raising this point.

state is greater and where large amounts of capital are available for money laundering. Hence, it is not surprising that in the periphery, where the state is weaker, drug traffickers organize private armies that, in addition to monopolizing coca cultures and cocaine production, become the de facto government of the local inhabitants. This is almost an obligation; if they do not do it, another private army will and will then have a huge military advantage in terms of controlling these spaces. Nor it is surprising that in large cities the state has fewer concerns about the degree of authority that drug traffickers may reach. There, the state has the advantage as soon as the money is laundered and deposited in a bank account that remains under the regulation of its institutions. The protection of the launderers depends on corruption, not on the authority of a private army.

A third critical factor explains why private armies have advantages over the state while ruling over local populations in the periphery. To a significant degree, private armies' legitimacy stems from the resources generated by drug trafficking. These resources bestow badly needed revenues and access to global markets on many pauperized, isolated communities deprived of capital, technology, and infrastructure. In this regard, the politics and war around drug trafficking in Colombia should be understood as the way in which peripheral societies access markets through the ruling institutions of private armies which, as a consequence of the criminalization of drugs, are better suited than state institutions in the periphery to protecting the streams of revenues from drug trafficking.

I deliberately eschew using a causal explanation that links state fragility and the rise of powerful nonstate challengers in peripheral areas. State weakness in the periphery explains why drug traffickers build oligopolies and monopolies of coercion. Yet, at the same time, the new oligopolies and monopolies of coercion impact the dynamics of state reconfiguration as well as drug trafficking itself. Controlling a territory may facilitate the production and transport of drugs to international markets, which provides drug traffickers with more resources to extend their territorial control through coercion and corruption. But, inadvertently, it may also prompt a repressive response by the state, which seeks to diminish drug traffickers' increasing power in peripheral areas. Such a response may lead to the destruction of coca crops and cocaine laboratories. In other words, it seems more accurate to talk about interaction, with potential different trajectories, than an explanatory variable.

In developing these arguments, this Element proceeds in two stages. In the first section (chapter 2 to 4), based on evidence gathered from extensive field work in Colombia, I propose an interpretation of the interaction between drug trafficking and the process of reconfiguration of the state. The latter offers an interpretation of general governance patterns in the periphery including (1) of where and to what extent drug traffickers' private armies act like a state, and (2) the nature of interactions between the central state and the authorities in the periphery – where the latter consists of both politicians and private armies. In Section 5, I focus on the dynamics of the reconfiguration of the state in Colombia after the cocaine boom of the mid-1970s and the evolution of private armies in Colombia – from the hitmen and death squads of the early 1980s to Pablo Escobar's gangs and the paramilitary groups that evolved into warlords in the mid-1990s (Duncan 2006). This trajectory is marked by the state authority's flaws and the offensive carried out by Marxist guerrillas since the early 1980s, both of which shaped the oligopolies and monopolies of coercion that drug traffickers later imposed, as well as the subsequent response of the state in the form of its attempts to meet its institutional obligations in the periphery.

Colombia represents a critical case that illustrates the main argument of this work. Arguably in no other Latin American case – perhaps with the exception of Mexico – have the interactions between drug trafficking and the reconfiguration of the state been more consequential in reshaping the ruling institutions of entire regions, the arena of subnational politics, and the process of integration of the periphery into global markets. There are references in political science to ruling institutions in Latin America that seem out of the central state's control. O'Donnell (1993) refers to "brown" areas where democratic institutions are distorted because of clientelism, personalism, and corruption. Gibson (2004) defines the concept of subnational authoritarianism to describe the monopolization of democratic institutions and of the channels of intermediation with the central state by local autocrats in the periphery. However, oligopolies of coercion in Colombia are a step further: This implies the organization of violence on a large scale to the extent that the monopoly of force by the state dissolves into a situation whereby a multitude of private armies share the rule of a significant part of society with that state, either in a collaborative or a competitive manner.

Next, I will mention some contributions of this Element to the literature of organized crime and introduce its methodology.

Why Interpret the Interaction between Drug Trafficking and the Reconfiguration of the State from the Perspective of Oligopolies of Coercion?

The idea of criminals as states is not new (Tilly 1985; Olson 1993). The state and organized crime show some important commonalities in that they impose taxation in exchange for the provision of services such as protection and order. Skaperdas and Syropoulos (1995), who introduce the idea of a "duopoly of violence," develop a model of gangs acting as primitive states in areas where the state already exists. While discussing the matter in these terms, these authors do not delve deeply into cases of criminals ruling societies, nor do they examine such criminals' basic institutions and their interaction with the state. Volkov (2002), Gambetta (2007), and Varese (2001, 2017) offer a more comprehensive perspective on organized crime, which they view as actors putting institutions in place to rule some social spaces while at the same time moving large amounts of resources and organizing markets. Their works have been essential to understanding the mafia as a phenomenon that goes beyond criminality and is also concerned with specific aspects of the government and organization of societies.

Recently, some authors have recognized the fact that criminals who organize the provision of drug markets and exploit other criminal rents in city slums are acting as local rulers. Auyero (2007), Arias (2017), Lessing (2017, 2020), Barnes (2017), and others have advanced the idea of "criminal governance" to refer to this phenomenon.[2] This new line of research has expanded our understanding of this complex relationship, but most of the analysis focuses on metropolitan low-income communities where gangs and organized crime rule over marginalized sectors of the population. A critical element missing in this excellent new group of studies is an examination of a mixture of two situations that imply a deeper effect in the configuration of the state: when criminal governance occurs in the periphery and when criminal organizations enjoy a high level of income coming from world markets. Doubtless, criminal governance by gangs in big cities falls into the category of oligopoly of coercion. But the resources these gangs can accumulate from the control of local criminal markets are relatively low when compared with the resources at the state's disposal. The income gained from racketeering, gambling, prostitution, drug retailing, and so on in local markets cannot compete with the resources of the state in the largest cities. The Maras in Central America are a clear example of an oligopoly of coercion underpinned by a poor economic base[3] (despite of all the mythology surrounding transnational gangs, Maras play almost no role in world drug markets). Like most of the gangs governing marginalized communities in urban centers of Latin America, which are dependent on local markets, their wealth is not commensurate to the coercive power they enjoy.

---

[2] Lessing (2020, p. 3) defines criminal governance as: "the imposition of rules or restrictions on behavior by a criminal organization."

[3] The myth of Maras as big players in international drug-trafficking rings has been dismantled by serious journalist reports. See, for example, Óscar Martínez, Efren Lemus, Carlos Martínez, and Deborah Sontag, "Killers on a Shoestring: Inside the Gangs of El Salvador," *New York Times*, November 21, 2016. Available at: nyti.ms/3Ocns9t.

If gangs that control the slums of large cities have limited resources to compete with the central state, the income available for oligopolies of coercion in the periphery is even lower. However, this situation changes dramatically when the oligopolies of coercion in the periphery rely not on the rents they can extract from the local economy, but on the huge flows of capital from world drug markets. In this case, the degree of authority exercised by criminal organizations over the population multiplies. Due to the size of illegal capital in relation to the available legal capital, there is a transformation in the organization of the local economy. A multitude of businesses that directly and indirectly depend on the capital injections from drug trafficking now fall under the ruling institutions of private armies. Furthermore, the power that the oligopolies of coercion can accumulate in the periphery from this source of capital allows them to claim ruling functions in areas where the institutional infrastructure of the state is stronger. This is a very different situation from that which has been studied in the recent literature on criminal governance. Oligopolies of coercion funded by capital from world drug markets imply a more complex transformation than the governance of poor communities in big cities; they redefine the economic organization of large sectors of society and impose new ruling institutions across the national territory to the extent that the configuration of the state is at stake.

By combining the process of state reconfiguration throughout the territory and the role of the drug economy in the shaping of ruling institutions, I follow a tradition in political science that studies the interactions between the holders of capital and the holders of the coercive force in a given territory to define the nature of state authority – a tradition that runs from Elias (1994) and Tilly (2001) to Boone (2003) and Reno (2002). In the case of Colombia, the issue is about the trajectory of state authority across the territory in a well-defined and consolidated nation-state. In the long run, the threats posed by the oligopolies of coercion funded by capital coming from cocaine world markets compelled the Colombian state to penetrate the territory and reclaim the ruling functions of society.

In fact, a significant paradox of the oligopolies of coercion in Colombia was that the relative strength of the state allowed political and economic elites on the periphery to take part in shaping the new regulatory institutions imposed by the private armies of drug traffickers and stake their claim to a piece of the "narco pie." The source of their power rested upon their ability to manage the state institutions that remained effective despite the drug traffickers' newfound power. With the exception of extremely isolated zones, the new structure of power relations introduced by drug trafficking never entailed the entire destruction of existing state institutions at the regional level and neither envisioned nor desired to replace the central state, unlike, say, guerrilla groups. Quite the opposite: The newly founded institutions in the Colombian periphery were really the product of a negotiated settlement between criminals, politicians, and local state authorities. Whether it was through agreement or confrontation, a new combination of legal and illegal institutions came to embody a new form of social regulation. In this regard, Dewey (2015) maintains that instead of perceiving the protection politicians offer to the mafia as corruption on a large scale, it should be viewed as representing the state's ensuring order is maintained in areas where the population obtains economic means and public goods (i.e., protection) from criminal organizations. States avoid conflicts, social unrest, and significant public investment by tolerating the maintenance of order carried out in an irregular fashion by the hands of other organizations with coercive means.

Finally, I want to explain the reason behind the title of this Element. Little attention has been paid to the subject of drug traffickers acting like a state in the broader literature on the war on drugs in Colombia. By focusing only on drug traffickers' needs for protection, studies on this subject have often reduced the discussion of the political character of drug trafficking to its impact on corruption and violence.[4] According to this oversimplified view, in Colombia, drug traffickers intervene in politics, whether through alliances or conflicts, with purely utilitarian motives. Once in the door, they threaten or corrupt the public authorities – using the logic of *plata o plomo* (silver or lead)[5] – with the sole motive of extracting maximum income from an illegal product. These studies seldom consider whether social domination (i.e., claiming basic state functions) could be the criminals' central purpose, beyond the logic of *plata o plomo*. Nor do they sufficiently take into account how some sectors of society may find the economic and political rule exercised by criminals to be in line with their interests. In this Element, I aim to fill these gaps.

On Methodology

Colombia represents a very illustrative case study because it has been the main supplier of cocaine to the world market since the late 1970s. More critically, however, there is abundant evidence on the existence of oligopolies and monopolies of coercion related to the capital brought in by drug traffickers, as well as a lot of cases of mediation between politicians or state officials and criminal organizations. Colombia also offers an enormous amount of variation at the

---

[4] With the exception of the works of Thoumi (1994), Camacho (2010), and Duran (2017), who consider the institutional dimension of the mafia in Colombia.

[5] This means the authorities are presented with a choice between silver in the form of financial bribery or lead in the form of the threat of gun violence.

subnational level[6] to test the argument I am proposing on the degree of capital accumulation as well as the appropriation of state functions by criminals.

To investigate the existence of criminal oligopolies and monopolies of coercion in societies linked with the production and traffic of drugs for the world market is a challenging matter given the clandestine nature of their activities. However, the ruling institutions of paramilitaries, warlords, and cartels in Colombia are visible to any casual observer who visits a small town or village where drug traffickers operate or live. The most difficult aspect concerns dealing with the core argument – that the less capital accumulation there is in a society, the greater the control by the ruling institutions of criminal organizations. Supporting this claim entails identifying changes in the organization of subnational economies – mainly in their patterns of inclusion into global markets – and the role drug-trafficking revenues and institutionalized coercion by criminals play in such changes. In order to furnish evidence, this Element investigates at least three important dimensions. First, it looks at changes in the ruling institutions, both those of the criminal organizations and those of the state, in several regions of Colombia, particularly in areas where violence was more intensive and where private armies imposed some form of control. Second, it discusses the nature of the political transactions between the center and the periphery to illustrate how democratic institutions deal with the power of drug traffickers. In so doing, it looks at four emblematic episodes of systematic corruption: the 1982 national election, the hunt for Pablo Escobar, the scandal involving President Samper's illegal campaign contribution, and the scandal regarding President Uribe's party links with paramilitary organizations. Lastly, the investigation looks at the transformations in the organization of local economies as a consequence of the injection of capital from international drug markets.

The investigation relies on four sources of information. First, there is a great deal of material in the academic literature on subnational societies in Colombia during the last decades of internal conflict and on the war on drugs, ranging from ethnographies and regional studies to quantitative analyses. These works offer valuable information for several regions and communities on political interactions, economic effects of drug trafficking, violence and, in broad terms, transformations of the local order. In particular, the data sets of some of these studies, which focus on aspects including variations in the institutional capability of the state, demography, roads, bank deposits, and coca cultures at the municipal level, offered a coherent map for the core argument of this Element.

---

[6] Giraudy et al. (2019: 6) emphasize the role of subnational research (SNR) in comparative politics by "offering new data and political units with which to build, test, and refine theories." This book mainly uses a SNR approach.

Second, this Element draws extensively on media reports. Journalists have done an impressive job in Colombia in terms of denouncing the links between criminal organizations and politicians and state authorities and covering the various wars arising from drug trafficking and the situation in the territories that are under the control of paramilitaries, cartels, warlords, guerrillas, and gangs. As part of this research, I systematically reviewed digital files of the newspaper *El Tiempo* and the magazine *Semana*, which are available from the 1980s editions onward. Other newspaper files dating from before the Internet era are not available online, but there are several journalistic books about the history of the cartels, the internal conflict, and major events related to drug trafficking in Colombia.

Third, testimonies published by people linked to drug trafficking (a genre known as narco-literature) as well as artistic productions (music and films funded and consumed by drug traffickers) are another important source. During more than a decade I have been an assiduous consumer of this type of material. Although the quality and veracity of these sources vary considerably, they provide a reasonably accurate notion of certain basic features of the practices of social regulation by criminals, links with politicians and elites, and their dynamics of confrontation.

Most consequentially, I conducted extensive fieldwork in Colombia over a period of almost two decades, including visits to zones under the control of criminal organizations and interviews with politicians and state officials, inhabitants of the communities ruled by criminal organizations, and people directly linked to criminal organizations (whose names have been omitted). Six former commanders of paramilitary groups in Colombia and five leaders of Medellín's organized crime structure were interviewed. Some of these sources were interviewed on several occasions, something that permitted me to dig deeper into questions about why and how criminal organizations rule societies. Allowing for the fact that the interviewees may have omitted a lot of information and may even have lied, these interviews were nonetheless crucial to understanding how the criminal leaders see their roles as authorities in a given community and to analyzing the nature of transactions made with legal elites at the center and the periphery.

2 The Business of Power Production

In contrast to legal capitalist enterprises, the production of narcotics does not encounter its most serious contradictions in the relations between labor and capital. Drug traffickers have no need to balk at paying lavish salaries when required, since profits are so much higher than costs. The problem for them lies in a different aspect of the business. In essence, drug trafficking specializes in risk reduction. A successful trafficker is one who puts merchandise on the market without being captured, expropriated, or assassinated. To do that they require protection, but protection is not cheap: A significant proportion of revenue goes to paying politicians, police, judges, private armies, guerrillas, and other parties with the power to either threaten or protect drug traffickers' activities.

As such, the major economic contradiction in drug trafficking is not between labor and capital but, rather, between labor and power. The exploitation of drug-trafficking workers is different from the exploitation that occurs in legal capitalism. Whereas a legal company owner assumes practically all of the risks inherent to the business, in drug trafficking the risks are also borne by those workers and third parties who produce, transform, and transport the product. If the business fails, it is they who must endure losses – a burden that often exceeds the merely economic and can affect one's liberty and even physical integrity. Thus, exploitation in drug trafficking lies in the appropriation of the added value produced by the risks that workers take. Risk is so pervasive that those who exploit these workers are not necessarily drug traffickers. Rather, those who specialize in the production of power – and consequently dispose of the means to protect, and at the same time the means to threaten – are those with the capacity to exploit the revenues produced by the risks assumed by those in charge of the business operations.

There are two main sources of power in drug trafficking. The first regards the coercive force of drug-trafficking groups, which may vary depending on the size of the organization, from groups of enforcers to armies controlling the population in vast territories. The second source of power concerns criminals' relations with the state. Drug traffickers bribe state officials and public authorities in order to protect their illegal activities. However, some criminal organizations enjoy more political influence than others. They are able to direct the state's repressive apparatus against their competitors, and to intervene more effectively in political elections and in the mechanisms for the appointment of public officials. The production of power in drug trafficking is therefore the result of a combination of direct coercive force and influence over the state authorities. And the greater the power, the greater the capacity to protect and extract added value from the risks assumed by others.

Viewed in this light, the political economy of drug trafficking and its relation with the trajectory of state reconfiguration in a given country hinges upon two major questions: (1) under what circumstances do drug-trafficking organizations acquire ruling functions in society through the organization of private coercion? And (2) how does the appropriation of state functions by criminal organizations transform the political relations between the central state and the periphery? The distinction between the level of specialization in the movement of merchandise and the movement of capital in each phase of the business reveals a great deal about these questions. Put simply, there is a close correlation between the geography of the state and drug traffickers' operational phases.

In the following sections, I will show evidence of the relation between the geography of the state and changes to the merchandise and capital variables of drug trafficking during three distinct operational phases in Colombia. With this evidence, I propose an interpretation of the ruling institutions produced by drug trafficking and how they interact with the reconfiguration of the state.

3 Merchandise, Capital, and the Geography of the State

As a business, drug trafficking involves a smorgasbord of economic operations, from planting raw materials in tropical forests to laundering money in cosmopolitan cities. These variations trigger sizable differences across criminal organizations' operational needs. Capital constraints for a coca farmer, for example, are limited to cultivating a small plot of forest long enough to bring coca to harvest, whereas a drug lord must raise millions of dollars in cash to transform coca into cocaine and organize its transport to end markets. For a launderer, the problem is not the availability of capital, but finding a plausible legal business to launder the money and insert it into the legal economy. Thus, the production of narcotics has a very clear division of labor.

A simple criterion for classifying the division of labor in the drug trade is the degree of specialization involved in each phase of managing the drug, either as merchandise or capital, in a producer country such as Colombia. The initial phases of the business, the cultivation of raw material, specialize in its management as a merchandise. The subsequent phases – defining aspects of cartel organizations, which convert consumables into actual narcotics and bring them to market – involve both specializations: merchandise and capital. The final stage, in which drug capital is brought to Colombia and laundered, lies solely within the realm of capital. This distinction in the division of labor has not been addressed from one important perspective, one that is brimming with evidence. A glance at a map of the operational phases of the business – that is, their geographical locations – shows that the division of labor in the drug trade between narcotics-as-merchandise and narcotics-as-capital almost overlaps with the geography of the state and the extent of criminal organizations' power.

In this sense, I propose three ideal types of state configurations in the territory: (1) monopoly by private armies; (2) oligopolies of coercion, and (3) monopoly by the state. In addition, I propose three ideal types of relations between the central state and criminal organizations. The first one is delegation, in which the central state allows private armies to exercise most ruling functions over the population; eventually, however, these armies accumulate too much power and become a threat, and the central state usually resorts to coercion to neutralize them. A second type, mediation, consists of negotiations between criminal organizations and local politicians and state authorities to define in practice the institutions that govern society. The boundaries between existing ruling institutions are blurred since coercion by the state and by criminal organizations overlaps and operates simultaneously. Frequently, negotiations fail and, as a consequence, the reconfiguration of these institutions is defined through violence. A third type is bribery, in which politicians and authorities receive payment from criminal organizations, but the payment under no circumstances implies the concession of ruling functions, only protection.

Crops: Monopoly by Criminals – Delegation

Several studies of organized crime have highlighted the role that peripheral zones play as areas of economic exploitation favored by the pirates, gangs, and private armies that operate in the shadows of the state (Skaperdas 1995; Gallant 1999):

> No states today and even more so in the past had the absolute monopoly of the use of force within their territories. In addition to simple robbers and bandits, there are or have been areas with little economic or other interest to state authorities to be worth extending direct control. Mountains, jungle, desert and other areas have thus been the breeding grounds of brigandage, rebellions, and independence movements. Thus, geography can play a role in creating a power vacuum that can then be filled by an organization that plays the role of a quasi-government. (Skaperdas 1995: 80)

This is the case in the fields of coca. They are located in places with little state presence, where criminal organizations take advantage of this authority vacuum to produce the raw material for trafficking drugs. Map 1 compares the locations of areas of illicit cultivation of coca in Colombia with the presence of state institutions. It is clearly visible that activities related to cultivation are concentrated in peripheral societies far from the reach of the state, and it is no coincidence that this is where crops are grown. The weaker the presence of state institutions, the lower the risks and costs that peasant farmers, as producers of illicit goods, must face. The potential losses due to state intervention are the risk of seizure of land and the working time that must be invested in crops, since farmers have to remain in a fixed place of production until the end of the harvest. Moving the cultivation of coca from one place to another is not feasible in the

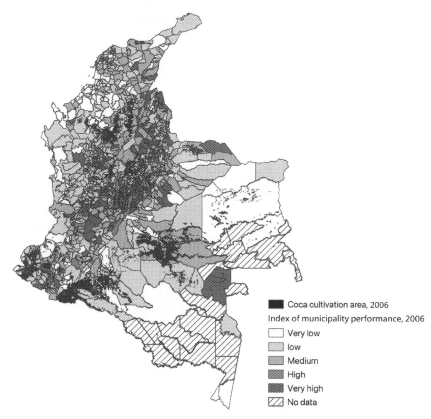

Map 1 Coca cultures and the presence of state institutions in Colombia
Source: Coca cultures, SIMCI; Index of municipality performance, DNP.[7]

short term. New land would have to be found and the ground prepared before planting and waiting to bring the crop to harvest.

Given the risks involved, property arrangements for cultivating the raw materials for narcotics are often based on small-scale agricultural production. This is because massive-scale farms involve unmanageable levels of risk for their owners. Not only are large farms readily observable from the air or through satellite photography, which entails a high probability of owners losing their produce and the investments made in planting it; massive-scale cultivation also poses a very high risk for the owner of losing large tracts of land and facing legal charges. The vulnerability associated with growing these crops requires the spreading of risk among numerous smallholding farms with little commercial

---

[7] I used the ranges of the municipal performance index of the National Planning Department (DNP) proposed by Garcia Villegas and Espinosa Restrepo (2012) as an indicator of state presence (Very low: 0–40; Low: 40–60; Medium: 60–70;. High: 70–80; Very high: 80– 100).

value in peripheral regions where state institutions are practically nonexistent. There, drug lords' private armies and guerrillas control the territory and decide who can work the land, what the price of the final product is, and who can buy it. In exchange, peasants must pay a percentage of their incomes or are compelled to deliver a part of the harvest to the ruling organizations.

In other words, what the private armies and the guerrillas do is appropriate, through coercion, the added value produced by the risks assumed by coca growers. Coca growers, in turn, reduce the risks and costs of state intervention by planting coca on very low-value lands, far from the state, where property rights are not institutionalized (Tobon 2012), and by receiving protection from private armies and guerrillas which enforce property rights in the zone.

Control of these crops quickly translates into the ability to rule society. The state's presence in such isolated regions is not strong enough to impede those criminal organizations and guerrillas who control the main sources of capital from imposing, as a monopoly of coercion, new ruling institutions. Inevitably, an alternative exercise of authority emerges when a monopoly of coercion other than that of the state comes into being. Permanent vigilance, the presence of armed men and the inquisitive disposition of those who control a community's ongoing activities are part of the daily reality of the new forms of authority. In his ethnography of coca cultivation in southern Colombia, Jansson relates: "[I] was always asked the same question every time I stepped off a bus in route to another village. *Who are you and what are you doing here?*" (2008: 157).

Moreover, although only a small amount of the capital from narcotics actually reaches the periphery, its effects on the market inclusion of local communities are disproportionately great. The state is intimately tied to the accumulation of capital: where the latter is meager, the state has much less of a presence. It is for this reason that drugs are cultivated in these areas. Yet it is this very lack of capital accumulation that causes the greatest changes in society. Altogether, the economic organization, the distribution of economic surplus, and the definition of social hierarchies are susceptible to dramatic transformations since the other sources of capital are relatively small. And the effects are readily noticeable. The community's traditional economy and ways of life sharply contrast with this explosion of consumption. Several anthropological or journalistic accounts of areas under cultivation offer accounts somewhat similar to Torres' experience in Putumayo, Colombia (2012: 58):

> There was a great proliferation of brothels, nightclubs and bars. A hundred houses, shops, canteens, guesthouses, restaurants, clothing stores, ware-houses, and agrochemical workshops arose. In sum, the surplus from coca was a great boon to commerce, whether formal or informal. From a purely regional perspective, the total per capita banking deposits in Putumayo grew

considerably: from 179 to 1,049 in Colombian pesos between 1995 and 2005. In a single decade, per capita deposits increased by 486 percent.[8]

A final reason for the predominance of coercive organizations on the periphery is that the state cannot extract resources from crops that have been criminalized by the state itself. Much less can the state directly organize the clandestine exploitation of crops. When the state eventually arrives with its institutions, the losers are farmers who cannot find a legal substitute for narcotics. As a result, the projection of state power into areas where it had formerly not been present is often followed by an exodus of people whose sources of incomes are threatened by the arrival of the state (Fajardo 2002; Reyes 2009). Not surprisingly, in these areas the state usually delegates the ruling functions to private armies if the situation is kept under a relative degree of control. In the case of guerrillas the situation is different, since these groups take advantage of their control over peripheral societies in order to accumulate resources in the war against the state. Consequently, delegating regulatory functions to guerrillas implies granting great advantages in the war, something the state is normally reluctant to do.

Middle Cities: Oligopolies of Coercion – Mediation

Unlike the cultivation stage, the intermediate phase of drug trafficking – which is controlled by cartel-like organizations – is a business requiring a considerable amount of coordination between individuals and organizations through a series of transactions, checks, penalties, and rewards in diverse locations and circumstances (Krauthausen 1998; Kenney 2007). The diversity of operations means that certain activities must be carried out in inhospitable places, such as jungles, mangroves, deserts, and across oceans and others must be carried out in areas with larger populations and greater accumulations of capital – both of which usually indicate a strong state presence. Drug lords, moreover, also aspire to live in places where they can enjoy their wealth. After all, what is the point in having hundreds of millions, in some cases billions, if you cannot happily dispose of your income in a place with an enviable market for consumption? It is no wonder, then, that traffickers prefer, if security conditions allow them, to live in comfortably guarded estates or suburban mansions. The perfect example would be Escobar, who owned the entire Monaco building, located in the fanciest part of Medellín.

Thus, the production of power at the intermediate phase of drug trafficking requires two things: first, the imposition of monopolies of force in peripheral

---

[8] Translated by the author.

areas where the manufacture and transport of narcotics occur; second, an accommodation with the political class and authorities in integrated areas where drug traffickers and their workers live and coordinate the whole business. In isolated zones characterized by low state presence, the imposition of institutions of social regulation mirrors the areas under cultivation. As drug traffickers control the main economic surplus that drives the local economy and use private armies to impose their rule, they impose a monopoly of coercion. However, the greater the number of cartels that operate in areas of higher capital accumulation, the weaker their capacity to rule. Here they have to deal with sectors of society that are not entirely dependent upon drug capital and with the forceful apparatus of the state. As a result, the production of power from private violence is not a sufficient source of protection.

The region of Norte del Valle during the 1990s and early 2000s is a good example of the various ways in which a drug cartel exercises its authority. The mountainous areas above the cities and municipalities were under the control of different factions of the Norte del Valle Cartel – mainly the Machos and the Rastrojos. Given its military superiority, the state could enter the area at will. Nonetheless, the state was not able to deploy judges, police, or tax collectors to govern the daily lives of the mountains' rural inhabitants. Here, the law was that of drug traffickers' private armies. If there was a robbery, they punished the thief. If there was a dispute between neighbors over property limits, they intervened to decide who was in the right. The situation was different in the main cities of the region, such as Cartago. Although the heads of the Norte del Valle Cartel had a great deal of power in the cities and municipalities, they were far from possessing a monopoly of force. Here, the cartel worked in conjunction with state institutions. Their hitmen monitored any unusual movement of men from rival organizations. They also had to ensure the safety of the population. And since drug money subsidizes the cartel's surveillance of the city, the population were not subject to any systematic tax. Similarly, many transactions were outside the cartel's sphere of influence. Leases and home sales, for example, were settled through state institutions. The parties signed a record of commitment before a public notary, and the cartels took no part in these transactions. Also, the politicians and the officials of the city governed in middle-size cities and municipalities and organized the provision of public services from the state.

Cartago and other cities and municipalities of the Norte del Valle region[9] exemplified a typical oligopoly of coercion: The state and cartels shared the

---

[9] I visited one of these municipalities, where I was informed about the history of the drug lord who had run the town and how he had controlled it.

ruling functions, while regional politicians and public authorities acted as mediators between the decisions of the central state and the criminal organizations. This type of mediation is crucial since it provides two essential functions in order for oligopolies of coercion to exist. First, it works on a local level in relation to the preservation of the institutions arising from drug trafficking and the definition of the limits of power between criminals and the state, that is, the extent to which drug traffickers with coercive apparatuses govern and the extent to which the legal authorities are in control.[10] Second, power relations between the center and periphery are mediated by a local political class that uses its relationships with the central government to offer drug traffickers protection from the state.

A clear explanation of how this mediation between authorities and politicians operated in the region can be found in a radio interview given by "Rasguño" (Scratch), one of the main bosses of the Norte del Valle Cartel. He revealed that he had consistently paid bribes to the police for their assistance in monitoring Cartago. However, he and his hitmen had to remain vigilant to ensure the police actually remained loyal:

Interviewer: So you also had control of the police in Cartago?

Scratch: Yes sir. And usually if I was in El Vergel, I had a checkpoint at the exit of Cartago and another at the exit of Alcala.

Interviewer: But who manned the checkpoint? The police?

Scratch: If it was a police checkpoint, I always made sure to have one of my boys on hand with a radio.

Interviewer: So you mean to say it was a police roadblock?

Scratch: Yes, you can rent the police – you just can't buy them. So if you give one policeman a hundred thousand pesos a month and another two hundred thousand, they let him through. This way, one of my people was always at the checkpoint with a radio. Ever since I've been there, all the exits were clogged with police and one of my people, 24 hours a day.[11]

In the same radio interview, Rasguño relayed in explicit terms how members of his *combos* (gangs of hired hitmen) throughout regional municipalities were capable of fixing local elections:

Scratch: He also told the village leaders who answered to other bosses of my "combos" that these votes, the ones they had in those neighborhoods, could

---

[10] In two personal interviews with paramilitary leaders, they explained that they usually paid a regular bribe to Colombian army officials, in order to be allowed to rule society and to exploit illegal economies.

[11] The information handed over by "Rasguño" has already been included in the character investigations conducted by the court. See https://bit.ly/3ba8zH3. Transcribed on November 6, 2013; translated by the author.

be handed over to "Flaco" [Skinny] in case he needed them for the lady [a well-known senator].

Interviewer: What do you mean by combo bosses? Did you have a criminal organization that also had a political component? How is it that combo bosses can tell leaders what to do . . . ?

Scratch: Doctor, [he interrupts,] in these towns, criminals become neighborhood cops. They get to say what happens and what doesn't. Each one of them meets with "El Flaco" and hands over to Flaco whatever people they have in those districts [to hand over votes to the aforementioned senator]. It's always been that way.[12]

A tacit and important part of the agenda for regional politicians is to protect the capital flows from drug trafficking to the periphery's markets. If they do not preserve these flows, they neither receive funds from drug traffickers nor the electoral support of all the clients who directly and indirectly benefit from drug revenues.[13] So important has drug trafficking become in transforming the political arena in Colombia that professional politicians on the periphery who beforehand barely had the resources to dominate the local scene now find themselves with the means and support to project their power on the national stage. They can aspire to a post in the Senate, to the leadership of their own political parties, and to becoming important members of any coalition of government. The "Parapolitics" scandal led to the indictment of around 100 congressmen for their ties to drug traffickers' private armies (Lopez 2007, 2010); most of these were regional politicians who had attained an important role in national politics thanks to the support of different factions of paramilitaries in the periphery.

While it is not unusual for members of the political class on the periphery to enlist the muscle and money associated with drug trafficking in their efforts to compete for power, one should not assume that they are simply subordinate to criminal organizations. Just because they advance the interests of certain criminals does not mean that they lack their own agendas. Like their predecessors well before the rising economic tide of drug trafficking, their main objectives are to obtain electoral majorities, control public resources and state agencies, and meet the needs of the clientele who contributed to their election.

---

[12] Available at lafm.com.co. "Alias 'rasguño' dice que Dilian Francisca Toro recibio apoyo de lideres que presionaron a la poblacion para que votaran por ella" (Scratch says Dilian Francisca Toro received support from leaders who constrained the people in order to vote for her). See https://bit.ly/3ba8zH3. Transcribed on November 6, 2013; translated by the author.

[13] Three of the paramilitary commanders I interviewed mentioned that bringing economic prosperity to the regions under the control of their armies was part of their military strategy. Prosperity was linked to drug revenues, since these were regions where coca fields, laboratories, and cocaine corridors provided the main sources of income.

In fact, the distortion of state institutions in order to serve private agendas often occurs prior to the arrival of drug trafficking.

Big Cities: Monopoly by the State – Bribery

It is in big cities, in the very midst of the state's largest institutions, where drug traffickers find the means, the specialists, and the economic conditions to carry out the last stage of their business process: to launder the money. For sure, it would be safer for cartel bosses to launder several million dollars in a small village in a forest or a mangrove that was completely under the control of a private army, but this community would probably be unable to absorb such a large amount of capital. Laundering the capital that drugs produce requires an economy with at least minimal levels of accumulation and movements of money. However, capital accumulation is associated with the presence of state institutions and its coercive agencies. The challenge in the final phase of drug trafficking, then, is to elude the might of the state – not to mention the problems of legitimacy, stigmatization, and social rejection that a new class of criminal tycoons find in the institutions of the social elite, the media, the academy, and civil society in general.

On the other hand, regulating the capital produced by narcotics is not an insurmountable problem for state institutions. After money is laundered, authorities and the political class are both likely to provide protection to drug traffickers without jeopardizing either state institutions or their control over them. In a big city, a cartel usually does not wield sufficient coercive power to challenge the state for control over the institutions that regulate capital transactions in society; and the state can regulate drug capital when it enters the financial system just as it regulates any other form of capital. As a result, in larger metropolitan areas, drug traffickers have to resort to bribing politicians and authorities to reduce the risks to their operations and for their own safety. But this does not give them anything like the concessions that they receive in areas where they enjoy an oligopoly or a monopoly of coercion. It does not include any rights to govern society; indeed, most political leaders are usually reluctant to directly meet with them. Several types of mediator take responsibility for reaching agreements and smoothing out such differences as do arise between cartels and the political class: Lawyers, second-rate politicians, public relations specialists, journalists, and other actors fulfill this role.[14] Moreover, the accumulation of capital and population in urban areas prevents drug

---

[14] Varese (2017) mentioned that lawyers frequently swindle *mafiosi*. During interviews I carried out in prisons, including some given with their lawyers present, some paramilitary leaders have mentioned cases in which politicians, lawyers, journalists, and other opportunists bribed drug traffickers, taking advantage of the latters' lack of access to spheres of formal power.

traffickers from forming clientelist relationships with the local population in order to control access to markets.[15] The sheer size of the market allows entry to large sections of society without any type of clientelist mediation.

This does not mean that corruption at the higher level is nonexistent in larger cities. On the contrary, there is abundant evidence of corruption among politicians and public authorities in large cities, including high-ranking figures in the central state. There are serious suspicions that various presidents of Colombia have received bribes from drug traffickers. Likewise, various prestigious companies have been accused of making their services available for money-laundering operations; even the Vatican's Banco Ambrosiano was embroiled in a scandal of this sort.[16] What this means is that corruption at the very center of the state does not imply the need to make any concessions in terms of social regulation by criminals. Unlike on the periphery, neither the social hierarchy nor the primacy of state institutions is threatened by such activities. As such, drug traffickers use bribery to receive protection from the state, but not permission to govern society. Conversely, launderers benefit from drug revenues without suffering anything near the risk levels experienced by those who actually move the product and exert private violence. The evidence shows that money launderers are also much less likely to be prosecuted by the authorities than those who move the product, and, even when they are, they receive much shorter sentences.[17]

Hence, the main outcome in big cities is a monopoly of coercion on the part of the state and the large-scale use of bribery to obtain protection from the central state. Nonetheless, there are two circumstances in which drug traffickers may play a direct governing role in big cities, close to the state. The first example occurs in some illegal markets where drug-trafficking organizations rule as a mafia. In the big cities of Colombia flea markets (known as *sanandresitos*) are common, and these are areas where smuggling shops (stores where people buy smuggled goods) are traditionally located. Organized crime operates a regulatory code there, but it is limited to these commercial areas and the drug traffickers who use them to launder their profits. Unlike in areas with oligopolies of coercion, where their private hitmen monitor the daily security of

---

[15] There is political clientelism in big cities too, but it is principally financed with public resources, the impact of which on the local economy is not comparable with that of clientelist redistribution in peripheral areas.

[16] See for example the BBC's report "Los fondos 'non sanctos' del banco del Vaticano," *BBC News*, April 3, 2012. Available at: bbc.in/3aJirYg.

[17] See the 2010 report released by the Transnational Institute and WOLA, "Sistemas sobrecargados: leyes de drogas y cárceles en América Latina," on the disproportionate differences in types of sentencing for drug traffickers depending on their station and position within the business. See: bit.ly/3PbCCgx.

the neighborhoods in which the population works and lives, the moment workers in *sanandresitos* finish their shifts, their security ends too. In the early 2000s, Miguel Arroyave, a rich drug trafficker, was appointed by the brothers Carlos and Vicente Castaño, the heads of the United Self-Defense Forces of Colombia (AUC), a confederation of counterinsurgent warlords, as the commander of their organization in Bogotá. The original objective was for Arroyave to attain firm control over Bogotá as the AUC had already done in Medellín, by monopolizing the rents from organized crime and ruling poor neighborhoods to prevent guerrillas from entering the city. Arroyave quickly imposed his rule in the *sanandresitos*, but was reluctant to enter the poor neighborhoods. The rents there were minimal when compared with the costs and the difficulties of subjugating the poor neighborhood's delinquents.[18]

The second circumstance occurs when drug traffickers' organizations use gangs ruling marginal neighborhoods to compete with other drug traffickers in the city (Duran 2017). As I mentioned in Section 1, most of the literature on criminal governance has been focused on the ruling functions of criminals in this type of social environment (Moncada 2013; Arias 2017; Barnes 2017; Lessing 2017). These places do not play host to massive volumes of drug shipments, but only the amounts sufficient to satisfy local consumption. Nor are they home to large transfers of capital. But their coercive power can be used by rich drug traffickers to eliminate rivals and wage war against rival cartels. An extreme example of the power that can be produced from these urban scenarios was the case of Pablo Escobar in Medellín.[19] In the late 1970s, the socioeconomic situation in the city led to a massive upsurge of juvenile delinquency throughout its poorer neighborhoods. Escobar took advantage of this explosion of criminality to create an army composed of young gang members that allowed him to challenge the state's policies against drug traffickers. His lieutenant, "Popeye," sums up the strategy: "While other drug traffickers were buying beauty queens, diamonds, horses and swimming pools, Pablo Escobar bought AUG rifles and R-15s, [which] the poorer neighborhoods were soon full of. He distributed his power throughout the districts with affection – that is, money and weapons – because he was an warmth guy who was good with people."[20] Over time his strategy was so successful that police could not enter neighborhoods controlled by the city gangs without coming under attack.

---

[18] See "La 'Oficina' de los paras en Bogotá," *Verdadabierta.com*, February 22, 2011. At: https://bit .ly/3AYp3gd.

[19] Two excellent narratives on the Escobar era in Medellín are in Salazar (2001) and from Escobar's hitman, John Jairo Velasquez, alias Popeye (Legarda 2005).

[20] At 28:50 minutes: www.youtube.com/watch?v=zzhyzVCDduA&feature=related. Translated by the author.

4 The Interpretation of Drugs and State Reconfiguration

As shown previously, in areas where state presence is weak, the inflows of drug capital may produce transformations in the very nature of power. New forms of ruling institutions arise in the shape of oligopolies and monopolies of coercion run by criminal organizations. Hence, the political effect of drug trafficking is not just about paying for protection or threatening to avoid prosecution but, more critically, about how power itself asserts control in a given society.

In this sense, an interpretation of how drug trafficking interacts with the state reconfiguration in a given society must answer the question of why oligopolies and monopolies of coercion run by criminals have appeared in societies where drugs as merchandise are produced and transported. A starting point is to interpret the production of power as part of the added value of drug trafficking, and the process of social domination as a main source of power with which drug traffickers can protect themselves. If the state and other legal actors are not strong enough to put a limit on criminal organizations' aspirations to power, those organizations compete with each other, to the best of their ability, to take control of the institutions that govern society. Being in a position of ruling over society ensures one has the power to control and organize all the operative aspects of drug trafficking as an economic activity. Indeed, when a criminal organization puts in place a monopoly or an oligopoly of coercion, it gains the means to control the rights of participation in the business. Whoever wants to produce, sell, and transport drugs in its territory has to obtain its permission and, obviously, has to pay it a share of their final profits.

But ruling over societies, whether by legal or criminal means, is a more complicated task than trafficking drugs. It requires the organization to provide services to the population living under its control: enforcing justice, providing security and surveillance, defining and protecting property rights, organizing the local economy, and so on. It also entails repressing dissidence among the population. Any inhabitant collaborating with or giving information to the state authorities or other competitors in the criminal world may be a major problem. In fact, in peripheral areas, a necessary condition for a criminal organization to control the drug business entails its ruling over society in a partial or total manner, lest another criminal organization establish itself and gain the upper hand in the competition for territorial control.

Criminal organizations can only rule – whether partially or totally – when their means of providing services and controlling the population can compete with those of the state. However, the relative strength of these means does not explain everything. The predisposition of a society to accept criminal organizations' domination also matters a great deal. A central aspect of the reconfiguration of the state as a consequence of the interaction with drug trafficking is that certain societies and sectors of societies find in the institutions imposed by criminal organizations a solution to their everyday demands for security, justice, and material income. For sure, criminal institutions as a form of government may be oppressive, and many in society may feel a deep sense of injustice, but these institutions certainly protect the inflows of capital into markets where consumption capacity depends to a great extent on drug revenues coming from abroad (Thoumi 1994).

Based on the evidence provided above, in this section I propose a model to understand why oligopolistic and monopolistic forms of domination exercised by criminal organizations in Colombia follow a logic determined by the geography of the state, and how this logic explains the interaction between drug trafficking and state reconfiguration. Before presenting the model, I discuss three aspects of power and drug trafficking: (1) the creation of added value from power, (2) the production of power as a process of social domination, and (3) the role of drug revenues in the inclusion of the periphery into global markets.

The Added Value of the Production of Power

Drug trafficking is a volatile business, full of uncertainty and threats, where even the slightest error can lead to a high probability of being killed or imprisoned. The typical way to reduce these risks is to pay for protection. The paradox is that any protection in the drug trade implies a threat. That is, you can only offer protection when you have the ability to threaten or neutralize other threats and, when needed, destroy the traffickers under your protection. The mobster and the politician offer credible protection only when they are able to subdue other mobsters and suppress the influence of other politicians.

Since the main threats to drug traffickers come from other criminals and the state, it is no coincidence that the two main sources of protection revolve around private coercion and the ability to influence the state. The Colombian drug lord Daniel Barrera, alias "El Loco" (The Mad One), summarizes this logic in one sentence: "Whoever doesn't work for me I kill or hand over to the cops."[21] However, the issue of protection cannot be reduced to neutralizing threats. Criticisms of Gambetta's concept (2007) of mafias as "the business of private protection" point to a number of attributes that go well beyond the function of specifically protecting diverse sectors of society competing for the accumulation of wealth and power (Camacho 2010). Krauthausen refers to mafiosi as "specialists in the accumulation and exercise of power. Power, in a way, is their most important means of production" (1998: 56). Yet, mafias have another

---

[21] See *Semana*: https://bit.ly/3B9SJXR.

characteristic that distinguishes them from other specialists in the production of power: They organize the provision of markets and oversee the use of violence to advance their interests (Volkov 2002).

In fact, most of the added value from drug trafficking comes from organizations that specialize just as much in operating the illegal narcotics trade as in offering protection and imposing market conditions through their power. In this light, drug trafficking is part of the particular form of capitalism described in a seminal work by Weber: political capitalism or capitalism dependent on power relations, which has been the predominant form of capitalism during human history.[22] In contrast with rational capitalism – the ideal type of modern competitive capitalism – in which prices usually are not very far from costs, in drug capitalism, there is an exorbitant difference between the final price and production costs. This difference stems from the levels of risk involved in the business, but also from the payments made to organizations that specialize in the production of power. Producing power, as well as offering lower risks, assures the control of production centers and trade routes, and the enforcement of contracts and property rights in drug trafficking. Any other trafficker who needs to use production centers, routes, or the enforcement services under the control of another organization has to pay for these services. And since power is a means of reducing their own risks and extracting the added value of the risks assumed by other traffickers, criminal organizations are willing to invest in producing it.

However, production of power in a society cannot be restricted to drug traffickers' organizational needs and protection. Power is the result of the interaction of many social forces in a continuous dynamic determining who dominates, who is dominated, and under what conditions this domination occurs. Those who obtain power do so for reasons that go beyond narcotics. Whether through material resources, ideology, military skill, or control over state institutions – among many other resources – the powerful are able to claim the obedience and support of many social forces.[23] In turn, such broad-based backing allows them to impose their decisions on yet more sectors of society.

Power as a Process of Social Domination

If producing power is central to the appropriation of the added value produced by the traffic of drugs, criminal organizations must develop strategies to produce it, either by increasing their military capacity or through their influence on

---

[22] The idea that drug-trafficking mafias are an example of political capitalism has been explored by Bernal (2004) and Misse (2007).

[23] For the sources of power in society, see Mann (1986).

the political class and the public authorities, mostly through a combination of both. But, in peripheral zones, these strategies fall short if they do not involve a direct process of social domination. Governing parts of a society with their own institutions provides criminal organizations an impressive advantage with which to transform their basic interests regarding drug trafficking into playing a role in the political decisions taken in society. The challenge, however, is how to dominate large sectors of society despite commanding an inferior force and fewer resources when compared with the central state.

More often than not, in strictly military terms, the private armies of drug lords are no match for the full force of the police or the Colombian army. The asymmetry is evident: Despite their massive power and wealth, drug traffickers cannot equal the military means and resources of the central state. However, in peripheral areas where state presence is shallow, criminal organizations may be more effective than state authorities in carrying out the basic tasks of government such as monitoring the population's behavior, extracting an economic surplus from local production and, in general, enforcing the laws that govern individuals' daily lives and interactions.[24] There are at least three reasons for their efficiency. First, criminal organizations have more information than the state about the population in marginalized and peripheral societies with which to enforce their institutions. Second, their ruling institutions are cheaper to impose since they do not have the constraints of the state – compare the costs of organizing a police force, a judicial bureaucracy, and a system of prisons with the costs of criminal soldiers who can act as police and judge and administer immediate punishment, from a beating to a death sentence, on whomever breaks their norms. And third, their ruling institutions are functional for markets that are criminalized by the state or that are informal, since state institutions are not able to offer property rights and contract enforcement for those markets.

In communities influenced or dominated by criminal organizations, acceptance of these groups' ruling institutions warrants satisfying urgent demands for protection, justice, and material security. Access to these services means accepting subservience to drug traffickers. Of course, criminal organizations provide only a type of justice that is advantageous to their own interests; and they organize markets while also exploiting them. But, however unfair the conditions of this domination may be, communities endure it as long as organizing some form of rebellion is perceived by the local population as too costly, dangerous, and unlikely to succeed. In most cases, injustice does not seem to affect social obedience so long as the dominated sectors do not find an

---

[24] This is the concept of state social control as elaborated by Migdal (1988: 22): "State social control involves the successful subordination of people's own inclinations of social behavior or behavior sought by other social organizations in favor of the behavior prescribed by state rules."

alternative source of protection, like the state or another irregular armed organization. Even assuming that people would prefer regulation by the central state, if the latter is neither willing nor able to deploy its institutions and if the people do not have the means to organize a rebellion, there remains no other option than to accept the status quo or migrate.[25]

While local populations may acquiesce to rule by drug traffickers, politicians might be expected in principle to resist the emergence of any competition for society's regulatory functions, control of state positions, and decision-making power. Nevertheless, in practice, large sectors of the political class are often willing to yield degrees of power in exchange for a share of the drug rents. How much power they relinquish in exchange for rents depends a lot on the means available to the politicians. Particularly, there are major differences regarding the means to achieve power between politicians from the center and those from the periphery. While both manage state agencies, the central state has enormous resources and coercive measures at its disposal. Politicians from the periphery, in contrast, have limited resources and coercive means, so they are more pressed and therefore more prone to negotiate with the criminal organizations that operate there.

Local politicians compete for the control of state positions in middle-sized cities or municipalities and use these positions to provide public services, seek rents, and distribute resources among their clientele to ensure votes for the next election. While doing so on the periphery where criminals rule, politicians and public authorities have to deal with the institutions imposed by drug traffickers' private armies. The issue is basically that of deciding the regulatory aspects of local social order that are under the control of criminal organizations and those that are under the control of state agencies. In exchange for allowing criminals to rule those aspects of social order that affect their interests, local politicians receive a large amount of resources from drug trafficking to fund their electoral campaigns. These resources do not only come in the form of money. Criminal organizations offer the votes of their own clients; local residents may collaborate with them in order to receive protection and economic rewards. Criminals also have the capacity to persuade potential voters by threatening them. And indirectly, politicians can count on the votes of workers and entrepreneurs who

---

[25] Nonetheless, opportunities to rebel against criminal organizations even arise in seemingly disadvantageous situations. In rural areas of Colombia, peasant communities without substantial resources banded together to defend themselves from guerrilla incursions under the leadership of paramilitaries such as Adan Rojas, Hernan Giraldo, and Ramon Isaza. The work of Moore (1978) and Scott (2000) on the moral basis of domination coincides with this evidence. When social obedience breaks down, it is not because of certain parameters of injustice but, rather, because of a rupture by the criminal organization of the moral limits established in the relations of domination.

own legal businesses which depend on drug rents to maintain the local economy and, even, those people who make their living from the markets introduced by drug traffickers. These inhabitants need to support the corrupt politicians who protect their means of livelihood from state prosecution.

With these resources, politicians obtain greater representation in the state offices and a greater capacity to influence the state and the political system of the center, both in bureaucratic and budgetary terms, as well as in policy decisions. In fact, part of their agenda is to mediate with the political class and influential sectors at the national level for something more complex than merely ensuring the protection of drug-trafficking operations and the neutral-ization of potential rivals in the criminal world. They mediate in order to preserve the social order and the ruling institutions on the periphery, both those imposed by criminals and those under the control of these same politicians.

If power as a process of social domination is understood as the ability to connect one's own political agenda with the social demands of communities (e.g., security, justice, and market organization) then the effects of drug trafficking on political power go well beyond the logic/dynamic of *plata o plomo*). In the end, the political achievement of drug traffickers consists not merely in their ability to bend political decisions in favor of their interests but in the very absence of decisions against them – an absence which is attributable to fear of the social reactions to such decisions. Assuming, somewhat simplistically, that two kinds of societies exist within a state, those who owe the satisfaction of their social demands to drug traffickers, *Sa*, and those who do not, *Sb*, politically powerful actors must consider both of these sectors' reactions when making policy decisions and competing for power. To further simplify the matter, political power can be divided between actors who fall into category *A*, such as the drug lords, corrupt officials, and politicians who consider the interests of *Sa*, and actors in category *B*, who consider the interests of *Sb*. Political transformations in drug trafficking revolve around the capacity acquired by *A* to impose its political decisions upon *B* through a combination of using drug revenues to win elections and channeling the potential negative reactions of *Sa* against other powerful political actors. The social costs of repressing criminal organizations can be so high that they eventually become a deterrent to *B*'s potential repressive capacity. This can be illustrated with a couple of common examples: An uncorrupted politician may still exercise only lax control over informal economic activities linked to drug activities in order to avoid major social conflicts; or members of a business elite that owns the bulk of legal capital in a society may lobby for a the prosecution of drug traffickers to be relaxed, in order to avoid covering the costs of meeting social demands themselves through paying new taxes. The absence of political decisions in this regard is basically a delegation of power from certain powerful actors in society to drug traffickers and political mediators for their ability to govern certain sectors of society in their stead.

This does not mean that drug traffickers' private armies represent a genuine expression of class struggle. The political struggles stemming from drug trafficking are, in essence, battles to preserve new structures of domination imposed on the periphery by criminals and corrupt politicians. The fact that this new form of domination involves the provision of social demands, and opportunities to amass power and wealth for criminals of humble origins, does not mean that drug traffickers are aligning their interests with those of the underclass. At the heart of the issue is coercion.

This notwithstanding, beyond its coercive capacity, the power produced in drug trafficking as a process of social domination responds to a great extent to the capacity acquired by agents – both political and criminal – of offering effective institutions for the inclusion of peripheral societies in global markets. Large sectors of society, mainly those located in places isolated from national markets or those which depend on informal markets, find in the ruling institutions of criminal organizations a source of protection for the flows of capital that maintain the consumption capacity of local economies. As indicated above, this constitutes an important source of legitimacy for these institutions. Hence, social domination by private armies is explained by the organizational solutions that, directly and indirectly, criminal rule provides to markets out of the state's sphere of regulation.

Access to Global Markets

While the relevance of drug trafficking in large economies like Colombia is by no means null, it should be placed in perspective. In aggregate terms, drug revenues in countries such as Colombia have never dominated the national economy.[26] They do, however, mark the difference between what certain communities can and cannot consume. To understand the politics of drug trafficking, then, it is crucial to note that drug trafficking is an economic activity that, despite being illegal, produces a valuable means of exchange in international markets for societies with relatively low levels of incomes and capital accumulation.

---

[26] Thoumi (1994) and Mejia and Rico (2011) have assembled an interesting collection of studies of the economic impact of drugs within Colombia. Even allowing for their skepticism regarding several methods of measurement, they show that drugs never account for more than 5 percent of GDP.

Stories abound of the extreme makeovers that have transformed the daily life of areas previously isolated from global markets. In Colombia, an ethnographic account of the effects of drug trafficking in the region of the Norte del Valle Cartel illustrates the impact on consumption in terms of an aspect as trivial as pet sales: "What's interesting is that up until very recently, there were nothing but mutts here. Now there are purebreds, even luxury stores and pet foods" (Betancourt 1998: 177). Of course, these transformations have also affected more significant aspects of daily life:

> Roldanillo has progressed quite a bit since the mafias came into town; beforehand not a single house had more than two floors, but now look: there are shopping centers, buildings, hotels, swimming pools, supermarkets and tremendous farms and estates within the vicinity. During the violence [the violence of the mid-twentieth century], the market was held in the town square with wooden tables and awnings; afterward, the Municipal Gallery was built. Now those in the Gallery are really struggling because the guys who run the show also own the supermarkets and butcher shops that are scattered throughout town; there are more than eight supermarkets. I do not know if they'll sell enough, but the capital they got to open them isn't as easy to get as it has to look as if you're doing things by the book.[27]

The importance of drug capital in the formation of peripheral markets is shown by the role that global trade plays in local economies. In their simplest form, markets are the result of what a society produces. A proportion of this production is consumed, while another is reinvested to accumulate capital, or gets exported and becomes a medium of exchange to import goods. If an economy does not have the means to produce goods valued in other markets, its consumption will depend upon what goods this economy can produce for itself, unless it has investments in other societies that it can use as a means of exchange. This is the case for the economies of large cities in the developed world, which are for the most part dependent on banks, trade, and services (see Sassen 2002). Despite their increasing deindustrialization, their capital accumulation enables them to become major world markets. On the other hand, there are politically motivated income transfers, in which the state redistributes resources from richer areas to poorer ones, as an alternative means of including peripheral communities in global markets in order to maintain a degree of unity over the country's territory.

Given the current diversity of mass globalized consumption, it is unthinkable for any society to consider self-sufficiency. Products ranging from those as simple as wigs and T-shirts to those as sophisticated as jets and Hollywood films

---

[27] Betancourt (1998: 162). Translated by the author.

now originate in vastly diverse parts of the world. There is so much specialization and such a degree of expertise that even the most advanced economies could never produce the whole range of goods that makes up today's mass consumption. Much less can societies with low capital accumulation expect to partake in global consumption patterns through self-sufficiency. It is for this reason that the social demand for inclusion in the market has had such a significant effect on power relations.

The expansion of mass consumption in all sorts of societies, even those with low levels of capital accumulation, is a global phenomenon. What is more, this expansion is happening at the same historical moment that access to post-Fordist[28] consumption is becoming the chief purpose of economic production in globalized societies (Lee 1993). When traditional societies gain access to mass globalized consumption for the first time, they incorporate new material objects into their lives that redefine their habits, norms, and values. Labor relations, romantic relationships, entertainment, and individual and group activities each acquire new meanings attached to these material objects. And as a consequence, criminal organizations gain an unprecedented opportunity to dominate in light of how isolated the local market is: They provide the goods that give meaning to social life.[29] Instead of invoking a sophisticated ideological discourse to legitimate their rule, the coercive apparatus of drug traffickers purports to fulfill, to a greater or lesser extent, the new consumption expectations of peripheral societies.

The effects of this Inclusion into global markets are reflected in two complementary transformations: a new social hierarchy that arises from access to consumption and a new organization of the economy. The new consumer products have a symbolic[30] meaning that goes beyond the purely material. Synthetic fiber clothing, appliances, expensive liquor, cellphones, the Internet, and other products do more than fulfill a material function; they help redefine social classification. Much of what goes into defining social hierarchies comes from two processes: first, the creation of symbolic value around certain

---

[28] Post-Fordist consumerism is the other face of the crisis of the productive structure of Fordism in the 1970s. Now markets are no longer strictly thought of in terms of satisfying concrete material necessities, such as a house in which to live, a car to take one to work, or household appliances. Rather, post-Fordist objects of consumption are designed to transmit experiences and recreate certain sensations in transitory and fluid ways (Lee 1993).

[29] With this in mind, Duffield (1998) has argued that the actual proliferation of political projects based on private coercion, such as that of mafias, warlords, and militias, are in fact coherent responses from poorly developed regions in order to insert themselves into global markets. Gallant (1999) also documents the role of illegal networks of bandits and pirates in the global diffusion of capitalism over the past three centuries.

[30] The construction of a drug-trafficking aesthetic obeys the need to symbolically appropriate economic and political power. See, for example, the work of Astorga (1995) and Edberg (2004).

consumer goods; and second, control over the distribution of these objects (Douglas and Isherwood 1981). In the case of changes to the social order as a result of drug trafficking, the new categorization of social hierarchies can be measured by the symbolic value of new objects of mass consumption. Drug traffickers are powerful not only by means of their powerful business but also because of their consumption power, which bestows upon them symbolic legitimization in newly created social hierarchies.

If traditional elites do not have enough wealth to compete with drug capital, they are at serious risk of losing control over the distribution of consumer products that define social hierarchies. As Appadurai (1991: 45) notes, "when rapid changes in the sphere of consumption are not inspired or regulated by those in power, they quickly seem to threaten them." In Colombia, new markets were created with global commodities, and their appearance in social environments previously excluded from these markets brought about profound transformations in social hierarchies. The ostentation of new wardrobes, cars, and other luxury items increased the social recognition of drug traffickers and facilitated their rise to becoming the new community "dons" by redefining the symbolic value of objects. Thus, the social recognition of the refined goods and austere forms of consumption that had previously distinguished aristocrats, bosses, and land-owners from serfs, peasants, and the lower classes was blown to pieces.

At the time that drug trafficking irrupted in Medellín, a local intellectual, Mario Arango, described the implicit defiance of traditional elites through drug traf-fickers' consumption patterns in a very interesting, albeit prejudiced, narrative:

> On a Sunday afternoon in 1987 I left Medellín with a group of friends on a tour of nearby municipalities to do the so-called eastern loop. When we stopped at a roadside restaurant for a drink, as is customary on such tours, I paid close attention to the other customers, the models of cars in the parking lot, and the customers and cars that were arriving. Most looked like what people would have referred to twenty years earlier as "negros," but their social status had somehow changed. Their demeanor was not that of a diffident people brought low and insecure by poverty and dependence upon a patronizing employer. On the contrary, these were not only ostenta-tious men who flaunted their superior and more expensive objects, their casual and flashy outfits and chests covered with glittering gold chains, they were also accompanied by better-dressed women – at least going by the cost of their imported clothes – but who belonged to the same class.
>
> (Arango Jaramillo 1988: 13)

The other aspect of how new consumption patterns are reflected in social transformations is that of economic organization; that is, the changes in what society produces and the role assigned to individuals in the production process, depending on the particular attributes of the social group to which they belong. In Bahia Solano,[31] a town on the Colombian Pacific coast, some young fishermen changed their line of work. They traded in long, strenuous days at sea on obsolete fishing vessels for short trips on up-to-date, high-speed motorboats carrying cocaine to Central America. If their new jobs were far riskier – crew members were frequently injured or killed by authorities, pirates, and accidents – a single trip covered the cost of living and spending lavishly for several months back in the village. Projecting mass consumption as a way to convince local fishermen to change their line of work was simple: Young fishermen were constantly bombarded by advertising for the kinds of culturally desirable products that drug trafficking had now brought within their reach. And apart from the effects of the new aesthetic of consumption – mainly seen in motorcycles, clothing, architecture, and entertainment – that reshaped the system of social hierarchies, the arrival of drug capital dramatically altered the nature of the economic activities in the town. Nowadays commerce and services, instead of fishing, are the main sources of production and employment for the locals.

Bahia Solano has an isolated population of just over 10,000 people, unconnected to the rest of Colombia because of its poor infrastructure. But even in middle-sized cities, the effects of inclusion into the broader market brought about by drug trafficking can be felt. During an interview I conducted with Salvatore Mancuso, one of the most emblematic paramilitary commanders who had presided over an army of nearly 5,000 combatants in the northwest of Colombia, he said that the press had claimed he was based in Tierralta, a municipality in the department of Córdoba that currently has 100,000 inhabitants. This was not true: "I went to that town at the beginning of the nineties only once. They were really poor. The town was in ruins," he said: "then the coca leaf arrived and when I returned years later, the trade there was astonishing."[32] In fact, the effects of drug money reached further than Tierralta. The economic transformation of Montería, the capital of Córdoba, was so evident that it attracted the attention of the national media. A magazine called the city the Colombian Miami due to the new shopping centers, high-end vehicles, and mansions that began to appear overnight in a city that previously lived on livestock.[33]

---

[31] This information comes from various press reports and personal interviews. See, for example, Jhonattan Arredondo Grisales, "Bahía Solano: Belleza y Desigualdad," *La Cola de Rata*, December 23, 2016: https://bit.ly/3Oxo9u0.

[32] Personal interview in Itagui prison, circa 2007.

[33] See "El Miami costeño," *Semana*, September 9, 2004, www.semana.com/el-miami-costeno /68382-3/.

The expansion of the tertiary sector with an abundance of stores and services does not mean that markets are entirely free. Clientelism plays a central role in the new economic organization and in the institutions of social control imposed by private armies (Gutierrez Sanin 2019). When a drug trafficker pays a portion of his capital to coercive organizations and the political class for protection, he is indirectly buying popular support through clientelism. Private armies and the political class invest in their clients' material demands in exchange for their support in controlling society. The availability of a loyal clientele has repeatedly been documented as a source of protection for drug lords against persecution by the state and attacks from other criminals. An example, Gonzalo "The Mexican" Rodriguez Gacha, who was murdered on the coast of Colombia, far from his operations base in the emerald mines region, had deep suspicions about the people in the region: "'Coastal people are not to be trusted.' Not like, as he emphasized, his fellow countrymen from Pacho [his hometown]. 'Out there, if they ever see me cornered, everyone helps me,' he stressed" (Velazquez 1992: 99).

To a significant degree, the legitimacy of the oligopolies and monopolies of coercion rest on the clientelist networks arising from a source of capital that determines the degree of inclusion into global markets of a part of society.

The Logic of Drug Trafficking and State Reconfiguration

Evidence from the geography of the state and the nature of power relations that are produced by drug trafficking shows that, despite the volatility of the business, certain trends persist. The type of dominant institution and the power relation between the central state and the periphery retain a certain logic regarding levels of capital accumulation. If we posit that there are three ideal types of ruling institutions – regulation by the state, shared, and by criminals – each type will have a different effect on the market inclusion of a given society. And this effect changes according to the society's level of capital accumulation. Poor and isolated societies may find the ruling institutions imposed by criminal organizations convenient in terms of market inclusion. By contrast, wealthy societies may find that the incomes of their inhabitants drop if organized crime succeeds in replacing the state as an institution of government.

Figure 1 summarizes this logic. The x-axis shows the levels of capital accumulation and the y-axis the magnitude of market inclusion as a crucial factor of legitimacy. There are three different lines that represent the magnitude of market inclusion of each type of ruling institution according to the levels of capital accumulation. The line of state regulation has a positive slope: The greater the accumulation of capital in a society, the greater the inclusion in

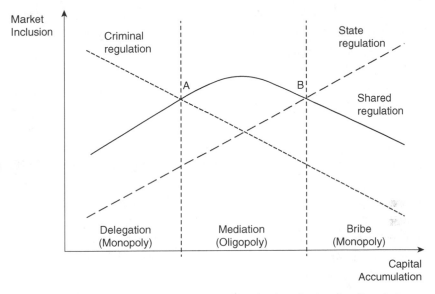

Figure 1 Types of state and criminal institutions by levels of capital accumulation

markets for the population when the state rules. The line of criminal regulation displays an entirely opposite type of behavior. As capital increases in a society, its inhabitants find that their consumption capacity diminishes when ruled by criminals. The line of shared regulation shows a positive slope up to a certain point of capital accumulation, at which the influence of criminality in the ruling institutions affects the existing legal business and incomes of the population. In other words, the injection of resources from drug trafficking does not compensate for the institutional costs imposed by private armies.

There is a threshold of capital accumulation – point B – at which state monopolies predominate and drug traffickers influence the governance of society only by bribing the authorities. This is because capital accumulation is associated with the availability of resources for society's consumption. If this accumulation is high, activity around supplying the domestic market will be intense and involve a wide variety of economic actors, and the population will have enough income at their disposal to freely participate in the market without having to resort to clientelism. Such availability of capital within a society ensures that the domestic market remains dynamic regardless of the resources controlled by drug traffickers and politicians. Furthermore, legal businessmen who owe their social ascendancy to processes of capital accumulation will prefer the state's regulation to that of a criminal organization. The state offers much better guarantees of their property rights.

Of course, societies with high levels of capital accumulation are needed to launder the income derived from drug trafficking, and certainly most of the drug money is laundered there. Some sort of protection is required to ensure that public authorities do not intervene in the laundering operations. Not surprisingly, bribing politicians and state officials is a common practice in the big cities where money laundering takes place, but in these cases, corruption does not imply that criminal organizations rule society. The payment of a bribe is restricted to the protection of money-laundering activities. Furthermore, criminal organizations may use lethal violence, such as murdering the launderers who do not pay their debts, but violence should be restricted to criminal affairs. Only in the marginalized zones of cities do we find some sort of governance by criminals who control the local retail market of drugs.

If businesspeople do not object to the injection of capital from drugs into the local market, it is because this infusion of income spurs further demand for their products. What they do not find acceptable is when the control of these resources threatens the hegemony of the state. Neither cartels nor paramilitaries, much less guerrillas and gangs, could ever protect their property rights as reliably as the state could. Any diminution of the state's regulatory capacity could mean the potential loss of capital for the companies that benefit the most from domestic consumption. In addition, the greatest strength of civil society in societies with high accumulations of capital is its ability to closely monitor its governments' actions. Media, universities, research centers, and other organizations considered influential in public opinion play an important role here.

Oligopolies of coercion are more profitable in situations of intermediate capital accumulation because they protect drug-trafficking incomes whose size related to that of the local market is considerable. In Figure 1, this situation can be seen between points A and B, where market inclusion under an oligopolistic regulator is greater than under a monopoly of criminal organizations or the state. In fact, because of the visibility of these incomes, operating clandestinely is not an option. Not only do private armies and corrupt politicians need to protect the business responsible for injecting drug capital, but they also have to impose some kind of order on the market. State institutions have no way of protecting and regulating markets that have been infiltrated by the drug trade, even in the case of legal goods. The additional costs of criminal protection and systematic government corruption are compensated for by increases in domestic demand. Without the distribution of resources from the drug trade, markets would plummet. Supporting an oligopoly is not just rational for the elites: Equally important is the reasoning of subordinated sectors. For the latter sectors, clientelism is a form of redistribution that ensures their economic inclusion in exchange for their support of the criminals' power. This is a central factor explaining the process of social domination by drug traffickers in these zones.

Nevertheless, at the same time, in societies with mid-range capital accumulation there are political and economic reasons for legal elites to be reluctant to accept a drug lord's absolute domination. If organized crime acquires too much power, elites can easily find themselves stripped of their control of public administration and their political power, subject to intolerable levels of rents extraction, or even facing violence and expropriation of their businesses. State institutions are needed to set limits. Otherwise, many businesspeople would simply abandon the area and take their capital to places where state institutions provide higher degrees of predictability. This, in turn, would debilitate local markets and, with them, consumption capacity. For the central state, criminal organizations that redefine local regulatory institutions are a threat and a challenge. But the state can afford the problem from a pragmatic perspective; ultimately, oligopolies of coercion are in essence a protracted state of mediation between the central state and the professional politicians of the periphery. Two factors incentivize this pragmatism. First, the state avoids assuming the political costs of negatively affecting the markets in the periphery. Second, criminal organizations maintain order and suppress other serious threats, ranging from social unrest to armed insurgencies, in peripheral areas, while the state avoids incurring the costs of repression.

Finally, in peripheral and marginal areas with low capital accumulation, the arrival of state institutions would mean the disruption of drug trafficking as the principal economic activity, and as collateral damage, the collapse of local markets. The *raison d'être* of the domination of society by private armies is to protect the main source of income that sustains local markets. Not surprisingly, there is a sizable difference between this and regulation by the state and shared regulation in terms of market inclusion, as Figure 1 shows, to the left of point A.

An indicator of economic transactions available for the Colombian case at the subnational level illustrates this point (Vanegas et al. 2021). The Colombian Superintendencia Financiera (the state office in charge of bank regulation) gathered data on deposits in bank accounts at the municipal level in Colombia from 2005 to 2015.[34] This database gives an idea of the movement of currency available for municipalities and that enables them to participate in national and global markets. When compared with information on proxies of capital accumulation like demographic density and national highways (see Map 2), it is

---

[34] Information available at https://bit.ly/3RF6gMM.

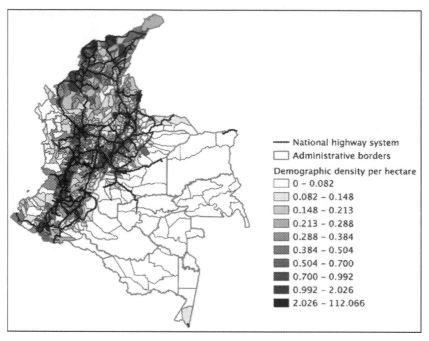

Map 2 Demographic density and highway system
Source: Vanegas et al. 2021 (with data from DANE and INVIAS)

striking to observe how a lot of municipalities distant from the main markets and the country's main infrastructure enjoy levels of deposits in banking agencies similar to those of municipalities integrated into the primary population nucleus (see Map 3). In many of these peripheral municipalities there is a clear display of two basic features: the role of private armies, as well as guerrillas, as a local authority and the importance of drug-trafficking revenues in the local economies (Vanegas et al. 2021).

The predominance of monopolies of criminals in societies with low levels of capital accumulation has profound effects on the role of professional politicians. In contrast with societies regulated by oligopolies of coercion, local politicians find their means of power too much affected by the capital and the coercion derived from drug trafficking. For example, in an area of coca cultivation, Torres (2012: 15) interviewed a leader of the Liberal Party who admitted his inability to win over the population within the logic of clientelism: "People from southern Putumayo had independent lives. They didn't need to vote because coca sustained them, not politics." It is not a question of whether the political class in the peripheral areas ruled by criminals will deal with the central state in support of the interests of criminal organizations in charge – they usually do.

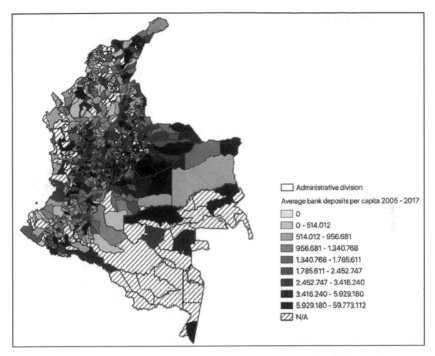

Map 3 Average bank deposits per capita 2005-2017 in Colombian pesos of 2015

Source: Vanegas et al. 2021 (with data from the Superintendencia Financiera Colombiana)

What is lacking in these negotiations is that they can barely count on state institutions to demand power at the local level because they are too weak.[35] In practice, either by omission or as a result of corruption, the monopoly of coercion conducted by criminals in these areas can be read as a delegation of state authority.

The model offers ideal parameters of state reconfiguration according to the geography of the state and levels of capital accumulation. In practice, however, the parameters of interaction between drug trafficking and state reconfiguration are much more dynamic. Eventually, the central state finds that the guerrillas are no longer a threat in a given territory in the periphery and, therefore, it makes no sense to delegate the authority to a warlord. Instead, the state, turns on its old

---

[35] The distinction made by Reno (2002) between the nature of Russian mafias and that of African warlords is relevant in that it runs parallel to the difference between the oligopolies and monopolies of coercion that have taken root in each of these places. Whereas the Russian mafia needs state institutions to produce wealth, in Africa the state is irrelevant for warlords' business.

ally, a pattern that has been apparent in Colombia since the 2005 Peace Treaty with AUC. Now, the state imposes a monopoly of coercion in many areas previously under the rule of oligopolies. But this is a particular trajectory of the reconfiguration of the state, in which the primacy of the central state in the periphery is consolidated. The opposite trajectory may also happen. A drug lord may take advantage of the power accumulated as a monopoly of coercion in a rural area to enter a large municipality and impose an oligopoly of coercion there.

Thus, in order to understand how the dynamics of state reconfiguration evolved in Colombia it is necessary to consider the history of confrontations and agreements between the central state and the private armies of criminal organizations, the role of other actors involved, like the political mediators and the guerrillas, and some structural variables, like demography and the state infrastructure before the cocaine boom.

5 The Dynamics of State Reconfiguration in Colombia

The state-making process in Latin America followed a quite different pattern from that of Europe. Centeno (2003) argues that the lack of international wars explains why Latin American states were restricted in terms of their ability to commit to all the population in a common national project. In many social spaces, the state never assumed its ruling functions, and violence was more a consequence of the lack of state power than of an excess of its repressive facet. In the case of Colombia, there is a significant discontinuity between spaces where the authority of the central state is fully consolidated and spaces where this authority is weak or inexistent, but where other armed organizations have assumed a coercive role. Gonzalez (2014) has defined this discontinuity in the history of Colombia as a case of "differentiated presence of the state." Soifer (2015) traces the flaws of the Colombian state to the historic resistance shown by regional elites toward yielding their local primacy to a central authority. In addition to history, geography played a crucial role in the discontinuity of state presence. The vast extension of thinly populated regions coupled with the existence of natural barriers hindered the integration of the population under the ruling institutions of the state (Gouëset 1998).

In the mid-1970s however, just before the cocaine boom, Colombia was, despite some huge differences in its territorial configuration, an already formed state with a central authority and clearly recognizable borders.[36] In some places,

---

[36] Pizarro and Bejarano (2003) and Gonzalez (2003) disagree as to whether this could be described as a partial collapse of the state or a differentiated presence of the state. But all of them admit that there is a central state, not at risk of collapsing.

its authority was complete, whereas in others the state infrastructure barely existed or was simply absent. At that moment, three circumstances favored the expansion and strengthening of the Colombian state across the national territory. Firstly, the National Front, a pact made between the Liberal and the Conservative party to share power, reduced partisan violence in the countryside (Ramsey 1981; Gaitan 1995). Secondly, the impressive economic growth over the preceding several decades had provided the state with new and abundant resources with which to offer public services, from social welfare and roads to justice and protection, to many inhabitants that previously had not established any link with the state (Henderson 2006). These resources were also instrumental for developing clientelistic networks between national and subnational politicians and between subnational politicians and the local inhabitants (Leal and Davila 1990). And thirdly, rapid urbanization facilitated the control of the population since it was easier and cheaper to deploy state infrastructure in big cities than in a complex rural geography divided by three mountain chains and endless savannas and forests (Gouëset 1998).

Yet, the expansion of the state infrastructure throughout Colombia's territory was still far from complete. Given the demand for new lands, the lack of agrarian reform, and the vastness of the territory, cyclical processes of colonization had been extending the frontiers of the country's inhabitable territory into savannas and forests without any state infrastructure (Molano 1987). After each phase of new settlement, the state would gradually be extended into emerging population centers through the building of new roads, the appointment of public officials, and the provision of basic services. Settlers who could not access land or who failed to settle in the newly developed zones continued the cycle of penetrating even further into more remote areas (Jaramillo et al. 1989; Londoño 1989).

By itself, the process of colonization did not pose a significant threat to state authority. The problem came later, in the early 1980s, when a group of Marxist guerrillas accumulated enough military force in peripheral areas of colonization to expand into regions more integrated with the national markets and the main urban centers of the country. The guerrilla warfare offensive coincided with the drug-trade boom and the emergence of Colombian drug cartels, new parties that contributed to the escalation of the internal conflict (Rangel 1998; Henderson 2012). On the one hand, the guerrillas acceded to large amounts of resources when they imposed fees on the cocaine laboratories and coca fields in the zones under their control. On the other hand, many drug traffickers were compelled to organize sophisticated private armies to compete for the control of the main traffic corridors and to maintain a safe area from which to manage drug operations. Monopolies and oligopolies of coercion run by drug traffickers became engaged, from that point on, in the dynamics of a counterinsurgency war (Ronderos 2014). For sure, even without guerrillas in the landscape, drug traffickers would have had to organize coercive apparatuses to compete for the control of the production zones and the rents of cocaine. Nevertheless, military challenges posed by the insurgency shaped the logic of their coercive apparatuses: They had to command enough coercive capacity to control territories by assuming state functions in the periphery.

Against the backdrop of a steep escalation of violence and armed conflict, the state was driven to bring its institutions, agencies, and ruling capacity to many regions where its presence and authority had been scant. In other words, drug trafficking and private armies extended markets and the demand for some sort of order toward peripheral areas, where later the state was compelled to intervene in order to avoid a worse situation of violence and criminality. During all this, the political class worked as the great mediator between the central state and the oligopolies and monopolies of coercion exercised by private armies that appeared in many regions. Recurrent scandals – like the Proceso 8000 and the Parapolitic – left no doubt about the role of the political class as mediator (Lopez 2010; Duncan 2018). But behind the corruption that altered the regional map of the political class and its influence on national politics, there was a setting of limits on the extent to which the state would tolerate the power of oligopolies and monopolies of coercion in the subnational context or their role as a counterinsurgent force and as rulers of the new markets produced by drug surpluses. On quite a few occasions, disagreements around setting the limits of such power led to brutal clashes. The case of Pablo Escobar is by far the most famous one, perhaps unique in its nature, but recurrently the state has sought to repress powerful drug lords when they accumulated too much power.

In this section, I describe the formation process of oligopolies and monopolies of coercion in Colombia as part of the logic of the interaction between drug trafficking and state reconfiguration, the evolution of these oligopolies and monopolies in the dynamics of confrontation with the Marxist guerrillas, and the reactions of the state and the political class to the different challenges that an internal conflict and the surplus of international drug trafficking brought about. I highlight how, in the end, the result was an impressive process on the part of the state, which strengthened its resources and means in order to display its ruling institutions across the territory.

The Marxist Guerrillas and the Initial Paramilitary Response

Successful projects of Marxist insurgency in Colombia emerged in the 1960s. To a great extent, they were inspired by the victory of Fidel Castro in Cuba, and was motivated by the logic of the Cold War. Despite being located in the periphery, in peasant and settler zones, isolated from state institutions, these guerrillas were not truly rural initiatives, but emerged from urban parties and political movements. The Fuerzas Armadas Revolucionarias de Colombia (FARC) was the result of the ambition of the Communist Party (PC) in Bogotá to have guerrillas present in the countryside. The PC took advantage of the existence of self-defense peasant armies, which sympathized with the Liberal Party, to conduct ideological indoctrination and transform them into its armed branch in the settler areas of the southeast of Colombia. The Ejército de Liberación Nacional (ELN) had its roots in a group of university students who installed a Che Guevara–type guerrilla organization in rural areas in the Magdalena Medio region. The Ejército Popular de Liberación (EPL), which came from a radical dissident branch of the PC, used a similar strategy in the northwest region of Colombia.[37]

The urban origins of these insurgency projects shaped the political goals of all these guerrilla groups. Although partial achievements – efforts at agrarian reform, credit facilities for peasants, and the construction of roads to integrate the countryside with the rest of the country– were relevant issues in the slogans and insurgency motives, there was an underlying maximalist goal: to take control of the state in order to carry out a Marxist social revolution (Giraldo 2015). The reformist sectors on the left were seen as dilettante activists, functional to the establishment and not real revolutionaries. In other words, partial gains for peasants had to wait until the guerrillas had won the war. Under such logic, the performance of the guerrillas in the 1960s and 1970s was focused on the accumulation of force from peripheral zones to defeat the state in a military confrontation. From these zones, indoctrination and recruitment among peasant and settler communities allowed guerrillas to build a strategic rearguard to launch insurgent operations and to kidnap and extort landowners and ranchers in more integrated regions. However, despite some eventual successes, their growth in terms of soldiers and resources was quite modest during those decades. In fact, they were almost exterminated in offensives by the Colombian army such as Operation Anori in 1973, when two of the ELN's top commanders and a third of its troops were killed (Pizarro 1991).

Alongside the project of making a revolutionary army capable of defeating the Colombian Military, the guerrillas had another less heroic but equally important challenge to fulfill in order to keep the insurgency alive: how to govern the rural areas where they had become a de facto state, or in other words,

---

[37] See Pizarro (1991), Giraldo (2015), and Rangel (1998) for the origins of all these guerrillas. In interviews with former members of the PC, the ELN and the EPL, I also confirmed the main role of urban cadres in the making of these guerrillas.

how to establish a monopoly of coercion. A communist model was unfeasible so long as the war against the state continued. The solution was therefore pragmatic. Governing the settler communities would include a mixture of traditional institutions of peasant-based clientelism with the authoritarianism of a Marxist organization (Aguilera 2014). As such, the guerrillas operated as a force able to provide order and protection in peripheral zones where, later, the amount of coca grown by the settlers would be greatly increased. Meanwhile, the state had little interest in creating infrastructure and bureaucratic organizations to rule this part of the country. The costs of ruling remote areas were huge, and in any case, the FARC, the ELN and the EPL, with fewer than 1,000 fighters each, were not a significant concern.

However, in the early 1980s, after a long period of incubation, the guerrillas were finally able to expand their operations into more integrated areas of Colombia. New guerrilla fronts emerged around middle-sized cities and municipalities. Extortion and kidnapping become a common practice that affected not only the regional elites, but also middle and small-sized businessmen, farmers, and ranchers (Sanchez 2010). Very soon there was a response. The army organized homegrown paramilitary groups to confront the guerrillas. Despite being poorly equipped, the first generation of paramilitaries was effective in its surveillance and in killing the guerillas' informants and supporters. Much of the regional political class, and even some of those on the national level, supported paramilitarism organized by the army. It was legal then,[38] and the concern that paramilitarism was incubating a new threat for the monopoly of force by the central state was rapidly sidelined since it was the only source of protection at a moment when the state was not able to display its coercive force effectively against the guerrillas' growing practices of kidnapping and extortion. Also, the first generations of paramilitaries were under the control of regional elites and the army, or they were self-defense initiatives by peasants in poor and isolated communities (Medina Gallego 1990; Romero 2003). Thus, the initial paramilitary response in the early 1980s was not seen by the national elites as a serious challenge to the state monopoly of coercion.

In fact, the Colombian elites, and society in general, did not foresee that a situation involving a relatively small number of Marxist guerrillas in the periphery and the emergence of new tycoons of cocaine in Medellín and Cali would escalate into a bloody internal confrontation lasting almost four decades. There was some concern with the fact that drug money was funding the guerrillas – the US ambassador in Bogotá, Lewis Tambs, even talked about

---

[38] The law allowing military forces to arm civilians was Decree 3398 from 1965. It was suspended by Decree 0815 in 1989.

"narcoguerillas"[39] after a police raid in the Colombian jungle in 1984 made clear that guerrillas were selling protection to cartel laboratories – but the state did not take decisive actions to avoid: (1) the military growth of guerrilla armies, in particular the FARC, as a result of the new resources available from drug trafficking, (2) the incipient problem of coca plantations in the settler and peripheral areas that was going to provide the guerrillas with a larger population from which to recruit and more territories to govern, and (3) the control that drug traffickers eventually took of paramilitary armies, transforming them from small vigilante groups and death squads into a confederation of warlords. The flaws in the state initiative allowed guerrillas to significantly increase the numbers of their troops during the ensuing decade. In particular, the FARC achieved the goal traced in their VII Conference in 1982 of building an insurgent army able to confront the state army in open combat. In 2002 this guerrilla organization had at its disposition 17,000 troops well equipped for a war of insurgency (Aguilera 2013). Similarly, the flaws in the state response facilitated the imposition of oligopolies and monopolies of coercion by drug traffickers, not only as a means of defense against guerrillas but also as a means of ruling strategic regions for the production and transport of cocaine (Duncan 2006; Echandía 2006; Ronderos 2014).

Progressively, the situation turned critical for the state authority in the periphery. The growth of coca fields created the right conditions for guerrillas to have at their disposal a growing population in peripheral territories, where the state had barely displayed its authority. These territories acquired an enormous strategic value due to the large amount of resources derived from coca fields, all the more notable due to the fact that the state was not able to rule in geographical areas whose markets were now dependent on an economic activity criminalized by its own institutions. From a typical Marxist insurgency challenge in South America restricted to isolated areas (Wickham-Crowley 1992), the situation was evolving toward a new type of war (Duffield 1998): one in which criminal resources were strengthening the guerrillas, non-nation-state projects of authority by drug lords were at the center of the confrontation, and the process of inclusion in the markets of the periphery were becoming progressively more dependent on drug-trafficking surpluses.

However, in the mid-1980s, the state's main concern was elsewhere, not located in the country's periphery: how to deal with Pablo Escobar, who had decided to make war against the state from a big city.

---

[39] See, for instance, Pilar Lozano, "'Narcoguerrilla' en Colombia?", *El Pais*, November 23, 1985. Available at https://bit.ly/3o2CaFr.

From Cartels to Oligopolies of Coercion

At least since the early 1970s there had been groups of Colombian traffickers supplying the growing market for cocaine in the United States (Gootenberg 2008). Some of these groups, initially small, without a great coercive apparatus at their disposal, and without links to larger structures, experienced meteoric growth over the course of less than a decade. By the early 1980s, they had become huge organizations and had amassed the largest shares of the impressive amounts of money that Colombia had begun to receive from the cocaine trade.

As usual when it comes to organized crime, competition for the control of the criminal rents was carried out through a mix of private coercion and bribes aimed at the political class and state authorities. Since the main two cartels were located in two of Colombia's biggest cities – Medellín and Cali – where state institutions and security agencies were present, private coercion was practiced only in disputes between drug traffickers. Assuming the state's functions over the population, such as surveillance and law enforcement, did not appear in principle to be part of the cartels' objectives. As a matter of fact, Colombian society became aware of a new class of drug tycoons not due to the political power they accrued, but from their overt bragging about their wealth and extravagant lifestyle. The luxury of traditional economic elites was overshadowed by the opulence of the narcos in a none-too-subtle ritual of status claiming. Pablo Escobar even built the best-stocked zoo in Colombia, complete with wild animals from all around the world. The zoo was opened to the public for free. But the opulence of the new tycoons was just the tip of the iceberg. In a subtle way, even small municipalities and remote villages found themselves linked into global markets thanks to drug revenues, and mass consumption altered the habits and the organization of economic life across the country, including such backwaters (Henderson 2012).

Nevertheless, as cocaine revenue grew beyond belief, violence and competition between criminal organizations became more intense. To produce more power was now a necessity for survival. In the case of the Cali Cartel, the bosses of the organization chose a collaborative strategy with the state to solve its basic problems of protection and control of the business (Chepesiuk 2005; Rempel 2012). The massive bribes they directed at the political class and the security forces, combined with their concerted efforts to avoid confrontation with traditional elites, made them the undisputable leaders of the criminal underworld in Cali. There were no oligopolies of coercion as such, but a great deal of corruption at all levels, from local elections to presidential campaigns. However, the massive bribing strategy adopted by the Cali Cartel had a more violent side in a part of the organization that operated in a very different social setting. These were the cartel's partners, low-level operatives, assassins, and workers from the northern region of the Valle del Cauca who, under the command of local lords, were the support base for much of the cartel's activities. There, unlike the situation in cities such as Cali, the local elites of small cities and towns had no way of competing for the flood of dollars brought by drug trafficking. Social and economic hierarchies were fundamentally transformed, and a new social order emerged (Betancourt 1998). Any criminal controlling drug profits – and the roving gangs of regional hit men these profits attracted – could aim to monopolize power and influence social interactions. So strong was the control of drug traffickers in the northern municipalities of Valle del Cauca that, in an interview, the former mayor of the town of El Dovio, who was a relative of the drug lord Ivan Urdinola, said: "Ivan, though convicted for drug trafficking, while he was still in power, he didn't allow anyone to plant coca in the region, because he knew that if he did, El Dovio would suffer."[40]

The Medellín cartel, on the other hand, chose a confrontational strategy. Dating from the mid-1970s, this cartel began as a group of smugglers looking to supply the growing demand for cocaine in the United States. By the early 1980s Pablo Escobar emerged as the leader of the cartel, and the national press represented him as a "Robin Hood" for his generous investments in poor and marginalized neighborhoods. Also, by that time, it had become clear that Pablo Escobar had set his eyes upon far more than material wealth. Despite leading a life fully dedicated to crime, he wanted power. The initial gamble toward fulfilling this desire was a career in politics. Escobar used his money to gain the support of poor neighborhoods through clientelism (Salazar 2001). He built soccer fields, set up markets, and even built a new neighborhood for the residents of Moravia, people who were literally living on a hill of garbage. In the short term, these local investments resulted in his election to the House of Representatives in 1982; in the long term, they would prove even more beneficial to him as these communities became his main source of support in his war against the state.

The majority of the political class had no problem accepting contributions from Escobar – either at the local or national level. Even up until the debate over *dineros calientes* (drug money used to fund political campaigns) in 1983, there was never any widespread rejection of the notion of drugs funding politics. Nor was that soon to change. A new way of doing politics and campaigning had been firmly established: It became very difficult to compete in elections without

---

[40] See Nelson Fredy Padilla, "Travesia por el norte del Valle del Cauca (III): 'La maldita droga acabo con la familia,'" *El Espectador*, January 28, 2013. Available at: https://bit.ly/3PaacmU.

resources from drug trafficking. A telling case of the political effects of drug capital was that of the presidential elections of 1982. According to various sources, the campaigns of both leading candidates, Belisario Betancur and Alfonso Lopez Michelsen, had received contributions from the Medellín cartel.[41]

At first, resistance to Escobar's emergence on the national stage was not too strong. The bulk of society's power players adjusted to the social transformations of drug trafficking. As with the Cali Cartel, national and local politicians received bribes from Escobar. But eventually, sectors of society opposing the cartel leader's aspirations for power and wealth appeared. The newspaper *El Espectador* was relentless in its campaign against Escobar. Similarly, New Liberalism, an offshoot of the Liberal Party, led by the charismatic leader Luis Carlos Galan, had an ideological platform based on undermining the relationship between politics and drug trafficking. The underlying issue in the collision between Escobar and the New Liberalism was a recurrent dilemma between drug traffickers and politicians. Money and support from the former were welcomed as long as some political sectors felt excluded in the competition for power. When some faction felt the other politicians were winning elections because of drug traffickers' support, this sector denounced the links of its political competence with criminals. Normally, the drug traffickers adopted a lower profile after the accusations, but in April 1984 Escobar ordered the murder of the Minister of Justice Rodrigo Lara Bonilla, a member of New Liberalism, because he had publicly denounced Escobar as a drug trafficker and declared that he should resign from congress. Escobar's war against the state had begun. For the most part, the start of this war was not the result of the state's repression of drug traffickers. In fact, President Belisario Betancur (1982–6) was against the extradition of Colombians to the United States and an immediate consequence of the assassination of Minister Lara was a change in this policy. Several narcos were extradited in the following years. Escobar's real motives were personal. He felt humiliated by Lara's condemnations and by actions by the traditional elite and the media that had ruined his political career. Notwithstanding, after ordering Lara's assassination, getting rid of extradition became Escobar's main purpose and to that end he embarked on a war against the state. In addition to the humiliation of being incarcerated in the United States

---

[41] The former regional treasurer of Betancur's presidential campaign was Diego Londoño White, a man who was very close to Escobar. Escobar's biographer Alonso Salazar, and his famous hitman, "Popeye," have also both expounded upon his relationship with President Alfonso Lopez Michelsen. Indeed, mutual accusations by both campaigns of receiving funds from the cartels were common.

to serve life sentences in a severe prison regime, for drug traffickers extradition meant the loss of all their power, wealth, and social influence.

Escobar's war was made possible by the organization of armed groups within Medellín's poorer neighborhoods. In the 1970s certain communities were governed not only by the state but by vigilantes, gangs, and criminal bands assuming the functions of local authority. In the poorer neighborhoods and newly settled hillside slums of the second-largest city of Colombia, a new criminal subculture had emerged. Anyone wishing to achieve status, respect, or power had to belong to a criminal band of some sort which, in addition to committing petty crimes, also exercised a modicum of territorial authority (Angarita et al. 2008; Martin 2012). These youngsters, many with criminal backgrounds, went on to become Escobar's army; they went from being casual, low-grade hitmen hired to settle internecine drug-trafficking disputes to being the muscle in the war against the state. One of my interviewees, who had been part of Escobar's army of bandits, summed it up as follows: "We were going to die anyway robbing a bank. Pablo gave us the opportunity to die declaring war on the state." The charisma of Escobar and the resources of drug trafficking transformed a typical big-city criminal subculture into a huge problem of oligopolies of coercion.

The most impressive feature of Escobar's organization is that he created it in Colombia's second city, where state agencies like the police and the army had a large number of agents and troops as well as a lot of equipment and infrastructure at their disposal. The case was clearly an outlier since Escobar, a multibillionaire trafficker, was able to impose an oligopoly of coercion in a big city that extended beyond poor neighborhoods. How was this possible? In addition to young bandits with territorial control willing to die for his cause – going from the power ambitions of a criminal to claiming legitimacy for drug traffickers as a social group – the collaboration of local inhabitants in the poor neighborhoods of the city was indispensable to putting limits on state action. If anyone even suspected of being a police officer crossed the border into a neighborhood dominated by Escobar's bands, they were detected by the community and executed on the spot with no questions asked (Duncan 2013).

The fact is that a large number of communities had encountered in the person of Escobar a means of material and symbolic inclusion, whereas the state and the elites were seen as illegitimate. The accelerated process of Medellín's urbanization overflowed the capacity of that city's famous industries to absorb labor. Furthermore, the manufacturing sector was plunged into a severe crisis from the 1970s onward. A lot of inhabitants solved their income problems through political clientelism and the thriving informal market that decades earlier had emerged in the city's downtown area (Hincapié and Correa 2005).

Nevertheless, these sources of income and work did not meet the expectations of a growing population, especially its younger members. The informal market and political clientelism were bolstered thanks to both a growing boom in sales of contraband goods used to launder money and the funding of political campaigns by drug traffickers. In such a juncture, the legitimacy of the traditional economic elite and state institutions plummeted.

The war against the state did not occur without various attempts to negotiate a settlement. The meeting in Panama between former President Lopez, Attorney Jimenez Gomez, and "the Extraditables," the name used by Escobar to represent the Medellín cartel, failed because of pressure from the media. This only led to an intensification of the war. Before long there were assassinations of any official threatening to prosecute traffickers; terrorist attacks; kidnappings of members of the Bogotá elite; and the indiscriminate killing of policemen – over 500 such killings took place during 1989 and 1990 (Salazar 2001). Poorly prepared to deal with this challenge, the state responded by increasing the extraditions of Colombian traffickers to the United States and by slowly but surely strengthening the Colombian National Police. In essence, the war came down to a battle of wills between criminals violently pressuring the state and wider society to prohibit extradition under Colombian law, and a state that was trying to suppress them using brutal urban warfare.

Initially, Escobar was able to bend the will of the state. The terrorist attacks had created a climate favorable to negotiation, and the kidnapping of family members of the Bogotá elite had driven Gaviria's government to offer "the Extraditables" a legal way out, which included concessions on matters such as the conditions and duration of confinement and the possibility of legalizing a part of their wealth. The terms of the peace negotiations were sealed in the Constitution of 1991 with the abolition of extradition (Lemaitre 2011). A few days after the signing of the new Constitution (1991), Escobar turned himself in, to be held prisoner at La Catedral. Yet this was a prison that he himself had built and that was guarded by police on his payroll. Meanwhile, the cartel continued to operate as usual, with traffickers still paying him their cut and the oligopolies of coercion continuing to operate in poor neighborhoods.

However, several events would lead to ruptures within Escobar's organization. If over the past decade drug traffickers had been thankful for the fight against extradition, by the time Escobar entered La Catedral, many of them had become discontented with the costs of war. What was the sense of being a multimillionaire if one could not live in peace? Drug traffickers began to feel nostalgia for the old days when it had been enough to pay bribes in order to enjoy the fruits of their wealth. Meanwhile, the Cali cartel, Escobar's archenemy, could still pay off the political class and the security forces as easily as buying groceries at the supermarket (Rempel 2012).

Soon after Escobar's arrival at La Catedral, considerable tension arose between the military wing of the cartel, made up of bandits from poor neighborhoods, and the business wing, composed of billionaire drug traffickers. Any spark would have been enough to ignite a violent turf war. That spark turned out to be the theft of $20 million by one of Escobar's henchmen; the fire ensued. At this point, Escobar was forced to choose between those who were fighting his war and those who financed it. He knew that whatever decision he made was going to be fatal. After he had murdered various drug traffickers, the business wing of the cartel openly revolted (Baquero 2012). Fidel Castaño took the leadership of the economic wing of the Medellín cartel, and with the collaboration of the Cali Cartel, organized a paramilitary group called "Los Pepes" to fight Escobar. Castaño could already count on a powerful paramilitary army in the countryside to fight the guerrillas, but the war in Medellín was quite different. It would be necessary to subjugate the bands that supported Escobar in the poor neighborhoods in order to defeat him. Nevertheless, Castaño enjoyed two great advantages: on the one hand, the resources of the drug traffickers from Medellín and Cali who feared Escobar, and on the other, the collaboration of the state security forces under the logic of fighting a common enemy (Martin 2012).

It took more than a year after Escobar's escape from prison – during an attempt to transfer him from La Catedral to another prison – for him to be killed. However, it had only been a matter of time. Making war against the state from the second city of Colombia was unfeasible in the long run. His death had profound effects on the dynamics of drug trafficking in Colombia and the configuration of oligopolies and monopolies of coercion in the periphery. As I describe below, the goals of Los Pepes were not restricted to killing Escobar. They were also planning to combat the guerrillas as a national paramilitary army (Ronderos 2014), to control strategic regions for the production and traffic of drugs (Duncan 2006), and to control organized crime in Medellín (Baquero 2012).

More Oligopolies, Even Monopolies

Whereas in the early 1980s cartels consolidated their domain over the exportation of cocaine to world markets from big cities like Medellín and Cali, the guerrillas expanded their presence in the towns and intermediate cities. With the exception of some kidnappings, the principal victims of this expansion of guerrilla warfare were not the elites from Bogotá. Those who actually suffered the brunt of guerrilla expansion were regional elites. Practically overnight, their capital was devalued by the threat of expropriation and their daily lives turned upside down by nonstop abductions and extortions. In turn, their initial response came in the form of organizing death squads and militias in conjunction with state security forces (Romero 2003).

This first phase of paramilitarism primarily consisted of bodyguards and members of the police and army covertly murdering civilians suspected of belonging to the guerrilla organizations. As mentioned above, in the context of the Cold War, state security forces began organizing peasant militias to monitor the movements of the insurgency and its collaborators (Medina Gallego 1990). Not only did security forces, landowners, and regional politicians support paramilitarism; many poor and small peasants tired of abuses wound up siding with the establishment (Duncan 2006). Peasant families frequently suffered a double whammy from the insurgents, who conscripted their sons to fight for the cause and demanded the provision of food to sustain the troops. If they did not cooperate, many were executed or displaced. Thus, peasants who were without large resources and lands, like Ramon Isaza in the Magdalena Medio region and Hernan Giraldo and Adan Rojas in the Sierra Nevada region, as well as inhabitants of municipalities ravaged by guerrillas like Gonzalo Perez in Puerto Boyaca, organized small self-defense groups that very soon succeeded in expelling the guerrillas from their zones of influence.[42] Despite their lack of resources and their poor equipment, these self-defense forces were effective because of their familiarity with the terrain and the local population, which allowed them to easily identify and to neutralize guerrilla collaborators. With the support of the army and the police, these self-defense forces were able to stand up to the military superiority of the guerrillas, who in most circumstances would likely have prevailed in open combat. Very soon, in many zones where these native paramilitary groups appeared, the guerrillas lost the social ground needed to sustain their territorial expansion and their offensive against the state. At the same time, some of these groups extended their coercive capabilities to the functions of social control. They provided typical state services such as surveillance and justice in communities where they had deep roots. As a consequence, oligopolies of coercion in the hands of peasants armies began to arise in some regions of Colombia as a response against guerrillas.

Nevertheless, in the long run, the spread of oligopolies of coercion came more from another source of retaliation against the guerrillas, one that took the form of brutal bloodshed. Drug traffickers had the resources and the will to

---

[42] In the Centro Nacional de Memoria Histórica there is abundant material about the origins of these groups.

make war, since having private armies offered protection for their business. In reality, the economic role of drug trafficking in peripheral areas facilitated the transformation of the private paramilitary armies from those created to protect capital, like the armies funded by big landowners and ranchers, into those arising from the monopolization of drug rents. If the production of power was a central part of the narcotics economy, the exercise of private coercion was an ideal mechanism for producing power. Before long, organizing private armies and regulating societies within a given territory in Colombia became not only a means to counter the threat of the guerrillas, but an instrument for controlling the drugs trade. By the mid-1980s alliances between guerrillas and drug traffickers were breaking down in the countryside due to the growing wave of robberies, kidnappings, and extortions. For example, FARC stole 5 tons of cocaine from Gonzalo Rodriguez Gacha, known as "El Mexicano," and forced him to create even larger and more sophisticated armies to contain its expansion (Duncan 2006).[43] The existence of a common enemy gave the criminal class an important opportunity to forge alliances with other elites and peasants who were victims of guerrilla expansion. In fact, many of the existing paramilitary groups, like that of Puerto Boyaca, led by Henry Perez, were quickly absorbed by drug traffickers like El Mexicano, who expanded the oligopolies of coercion into many other regions in Colombia (Gonzalez et al. 2003). Also, regional political leaders and state security forces were quick to join forces with these drug traffickers in order to confront guerrillas and the sectors suspected of having close ties to them, such as the Patriotic Union (UP), a left-wing political party that had emerged in 1984 during a peace negotiation under the government of Betancur (Dudley 2008).

A particular region where oligopolies of coercion by drug traffickers expanded was that of the Eastern Plains (Llanos Orientales). The geography of this zone, characterized by a low level both of state presence and of capital accumulation, made it ideal to install cocaine laboratories and coca fields. When drug trafficking arrived, there was already an abundance of criminal organizations with the ability to take charge of social regulation. The emerald-producing mafias of Boyacá had decades of experience controlling emerald-producing municipalities with their private armies (Uribe Alarcon 1992; Claver Tellez 1993). From the mining areas, they extended their influence southward into the lowlands of the eastern plains where the authority of the state was precarious at best. As soon as the late 1970s, laboratories for processing cocaine were set up in the isolated regions surrounding the Llanos Orientales. Tranquilandia and

---

[43] While visiting a prison, I encountered by chance the guerrilla commander who stole the 5 tons of cocaine from El Mexicano. He corroborated my view that this event marked the beginning of the military confrontation between drug traffickers and FARC.

Villa Coca were only two documented cases in an empire consisting of huge complexes that could produce several tons of cocaine on a monthly basis. Though laboratories were protected by FARC – at least until FARC changed its mind and began to steal from the cartels – the emerald-producing mafias were important in monopolizing coercion in the areas immediately outside of guerrilla control (Henderson 2012).

Another important case of a monopoly of coercion installed by a drug lord was that of Fidel Castaño, the same leader of the Pepes, in the south of Córdoba (Sanchez 2010). His criminal history actually began in the mid-1970s when he became involved in drug trafficking with the Medellín cartel. After becoming a tycoon, he returned to his native town of Antioquia. At that time the guerrillas were expanding through the outlying areas. To finance their operations they kidnapped wealthy landowners, politicians, and other local notables, many of whom were drug traffickers or their relatives. The father of the Castaño brothers was a case in point. After paying a ransom, Fidel and his brothers learned that their father had died in captivity. Their response was to take a cruel revenge against anyone in the region suspected of having anything to do with the guerrillas (Ronderos 2014). Though the initial aim was pure revenge, it was not long before their personal vendetta was overwhelmed by the desire to seize territorial control for drug trafficking. Castaño acquired a hacienda in Córdoba – hundreds of miles from his homeland – and began to expand his control into the region of Urabá (Civico 2010). After expelling guerrillas from the area and imposing a de facto monopoly of coercion upon it, the Castaño brothers were rewarded with the control of drug routes leading straight to the Caribbean.

In the following decade the creation of private armies by drug traffickers intensified. Many paramilitary groups surfaced in many other parts of Colombia where drug traffickers purchased land (Reyes 2009). The use of paramilitaries as a means of controlling drug revenues, in the form of oligopolies and monopolies of coercion, was too often tolerated and promoted by local elites and state security forces because of their role in containing the guerrillas without the state having to pay. Neither did the professional politicians suffer the oppressive effects of the control imposed by paramilitaries in the peripheral areas. As long as they did not have links with left-wing parties or human rights organizations, and were not suspected of being sympathizers of insurgency, they were able to compete for votes and state appointments and keep their influence in regional decisions. Also, in providing security and social welfare, many paramilitary groups obtained some level of legitimacy and a lot of collaboration from the community.

But, after its rapid expansion throughout the 1980s, the phenomenon of paramilitaries in Colombia stalled in the early 1990s. Most of the first organizations were relatively small groups without any pretentions to acting like a state. Their purpose was limited to protecting politicians, landowners, ranchers, and regional elites from the guerrillas. Also, they were scattered and had no overarching leadership to coordinate their actions.[44] On the other hand, the big paramilitary armies, like those of Perez in Puerto Boyaca and of Castaño in Córdoba, barely expanded during the period between 1990 and 1994. The central state's war against Escobar affected the protection that the big paramilitary armies enjoyed from the security agencies,[45] since they were linked with political murders and drug operations for the Medellín cartel. At that time, the map of the configuration of the state in the periphery was composed of (1) zones of strategic rearguard where the guerrilla had monopolies of coercion; (2) zones of oligopolies and monopolies of coercion by big paramilitary armies deeply involved in drug trafficking; (3) zones of oligopolies of coercion by paramilitaries armies led by local peasants like Ramon Isaza, Hernan Giraldo and Adan Rojas, some of them linked to drugs operations; and (4) zones where small paramilitary armies acted as the bodyguards of local elites – politicians, landowners, businessmen, and so on – without pretending to assume ruling functions.

Corruption as a Means of Dealing with Oligopolies of Coercion

What were the national elites and the political class thinking about the proliferation of oligopolies and monopolies of coercion in the early 1990s? What kind of decisions did they take? At the time many claimed – hyperbolically – in Colombia and abroad that the country could turn into a failed state, but certainly the sovereignty of the central state in Colombia was not at stake (Pizarro and Bejarano 2003). The problem was serious, although it was of a different nature. On the one hand, Escobar had brought the war to cities and thus impacted the lives of national elites, a group that had never before felt the brunt of violence or seen its own power in peril. Once the state finally neutralized Escobar in 1993, this problem was greatly reduced. On the other hand, the state's historical failure to provide order and protection on the periphery became even more apparent with the expansion of the guerrillas, the proliferation of coca fields, and the growing exercise of power and coercive apparatuses of drug traffickers at the regional level. Although areas where the conflict with guerrillas was most

---

[44] In separate interviews with two paramilitary commanders, Salvatore Mancuso and Rodrigo Perez, they informed me that their first groups had consisted of less than ten armed men. They did not have rifles, only light weapons such as small guns. As such, they were pure defensive organizations. Several accounts from this first generation of paramilitaries, initially not linked with drug traffickers, confirmed their statements.

[45] This situation changed dramatically after Fidel Castaño broke ranks with the drug kingpin Escobar in 1991 and struck a deal with the police, a move that played a critical role in Escobar's killing in 1993.

intense did not pose strategic threats to the survival of the state, the violence forced the state into meeting its public obligations on the margins of its territory. To fail to fulfill these obligations was to run the risk of the insurgency and the private armies of drug traffickers spreading to areas nearer the center. In the days prior to the expansion of the insurgency and the influx of drug money, the state had no pressing need to invest more resources in bringing its institutions and infrastructure to the periphery. Instead, Bogotá elites had been more or less committed to a gradual process of the inclusion of peripheral territories through public investments managed by regional politicians. But the new security problems led to an increase in the resources, development plans, and public policies these politicians invested in integrating the periphery's population into state institutions.[46]

For many members of the subnational political class, these resources presented a golden opportunity to strengthen their clientelist networks. Hefty resources were utilized to alleviate the effects of conflict and social unrest, something that coincided with an effort to decentralize the political system. As of 1988, governors and majors were no longer appointed by the president but were locally elected. Then, starting with the Constitution of 1991, a larger portion of the state budget was assigned directly to local governments. As a result of those institutional changes, the balance of power within the political system underwent significant alterations. The states' resources were no longer concentrated in the hands of the national executive branch. Now, local politicians could access to public resources directly in the subnational governments to feed their clientelistic bases. The discipline imposed by regional caciques who controlled the flow of resources from the central state to local government fell apart when grassroots politicians were able to access them without that mediation (Pizarro 2002). For politicians aspiring to national positions, like the presidency or a seat in the Senate, the costs of obtaining the support of the regional political class for an election went up as the market of local politicians became more competitive.

An unexpected consequence of decentralization was the expansion of armed clientelism by guerrillas and paramilitaries (Eaton 2006), as well as an opportunity for politicians to negotiate protection for drug traffickers and their private armies in exchange for money and votes (Sanchez and Chacon 2005). The fact was that many politicians at the subnational level did not have sufficient resources to compete with those candidates supported by drug traffickers. Many second-tier professional politicians who had never dreamed of competing

---

[46] There have been a number of plans for this purpose devised by almost all the governments that have been in power since Barco's presidency (1986–90): these have included PNR, Plan Colombia, and Seguridad Democrática. For a review of all these plans see Lopez (2016).

with long-standing political caciques now found they were able to challenge them (Duncan 2006). Many of them turned into important national electors. Also, many traditional politicians in the regions, and even some at the national level, were now faced with the reality that if they did not accept the support of drug traffickers their chances of being competitive in elections would fall dramatically.

When subnational politicians in Colombia received money and military support on the part of drug traffickers, and the national government received the backing of these same politicians in congress, a transaction far more complex than the exchange of bribes for perks was now underway. Although on the surface most politicians had little in mind other than the opportunity to personally benefit from an illegal transaction, their actions led to a range of implicit and explicit agreements on the reconfiguration of the state across the territory. These agreements involved: (1) the degree to which armed organizations that controlled drug trafficking were going to obtain direct rule over local populations with their own coercive institutions; and (2) redrawing the architecture of power in the periphery, to determine the new positions of power occupied by drug traffickers, the central state, and more critically, the regional politicians who now enjoyed access to extra resources with which to compete even in the national political arena. As such, corruption was merely part of the agreements in the realm of formal democratic institutions that defined the limits of power over local order between politicians and criminals. These limits, for sure, were not only defined by political agreements; coercion from the state and from private armies recurrently played a significant role.

The new balance of power between the central state, professional politicians, and the criminal organizations that emerged after decentralization was reflected in recurring scandals. In 1994, a scandal broke out when it became known that the Cali Cartel had financed the campaign of President Ernesto Samper (1994–8). While Samper remained in office despite the evidence against him, the Cali Cartel's vast network of corruption – which included senators, famous party leaders, ministers, and so on – was exposed, discrediting many politicians and sending some behind bars.[47] Samper was motivated to accept at least $6 million from the Cali Cartel as he was under pressure to avoid an imminent defeat by the conservative candidate Andres Pastrana in the second electoral round. As usual, charges of corruption by drug traffickers came from those parts of the political sector that were excluded from positions of power in the state. But in all likelihood the deal between Samper and the Cali Cartel was more than just funding for a political coalition that could

---

[47] For a list of the politicians linked to the Proceso 8000, see Duncan (2018).

assure protection for bosses and drug operations once in power. According to some media reports,[48] Samper planned to initiate a peace process whereby drug traffickers associated with the Cali Cartel would submit to the justice system in exchange for lighter sentences, legalization of part of their wealth, and shorter prison terms. This plan never had a chance after the scandal. Yet, an additional factor hampered its implementation. Other drug traffickers, who had also made alliances with the state during the war with Escobar, saw corruption as a means to expand their territorial control and increase their drug-trafficking revenues. The partners of the cartel of Cali in the northern part of the Valle del Cauca, known as the Norte del Valle Cartel, rejected the submission proposal put forth by the bosses of the Cali Cartel. Instead of planning their retirement from drug-trafficking activities, they consolidated the oligopolies of coercion in regions that had historically been under their control and even expanded their control into Cali itself.[49]

During those same years, the Castaño brothers, the same dissidents of the Medellín cartel who had created the Pepes, developed even more ambitious plans. Their vision was of the creation of sophisticated paramilitary armies capable of expelling the guerrillas from entire regions and then fully taking on the role of the state. After a decade, this military gamble would prove so successful that it became impossible for the political class to hide their links with the new power of drug trafficking in the periphery. The scandal, known as "Parapolitics," would be far worse than the "Proceso 8000" debacle.

Warlords

Less than two months after Escobar's death at the end of 1993, Fidel Castaño was assassinated. Carlos and Vicente, the Castaño brothers who survived Fidel, then planned the construction of an army so superior to its predecessors in terms of its men and military capacity that its territorial expansion throughout the country would swallow the small paramilitary armies of each region (Duncan 2006). The logic was simple: The new army would arrive and ask the smaller paramilitary groups to surrender their men and weapons.[50]

The Castaño family thus embarked on an ambitious project seeking the transformation of early paramilitarism into a more sophisticated warlordism.

---

[48] See Vargas et al. (1996), for instance.

[49] In an interview with a former Cali gang member I was informed that "Varela,", one of the drug lords of the Norte del Valle cartel, transformed the poor local gangs in their private army in order to take control of the city in the early 1990s.

[50] This plan was confirmed in interviews with several former AUC commanders. Furthermore, a close advisor of Carlos Castaño confirmed to me that at the end Castaño's plan had been to negotiate a peace agreement with the state not as a drug lord, but as a counterinsurgent liberator.

This move was predicated upon two main pillars: (1) the significant military capability attained by the new private armies; (2) the ascendancy of warlords, as specialists in violence, over landowners, drug traffickers, and regional elites, who financed the paramilitary groups without directly leading the war; (3) the impressive territorial expansion of these armies, which allowed them to impose their own law and order; and (4) the large amounts of income they directly controlled, which made them independent of the need for third parties to finance their armies (Duncan 2006). Very soon, warlords had transformed previous forms of social domination by paramilitaries and increased their control of drug-trafficking revenues. As a consequence, the processes of inclusion in the markets deepened with the arrival of more resources from drugs to the peripheral zones which warlords inhabited and ran as parallel states. For the state security forces, the expansion of these armies was not seen as a problem, as the advance of guerrillas led alliances to fight a common enemy. Not surprisingly, during the next decade, the allegations by human rights organizations of collusion between state security forces and Castaño's private armies were countless.[51]

At their peak, oligopolies and monopolies of coercion had not only reached a new level in the periphery; even in mid-sized cities like Montería, Barrancabermeja and Villavicencio, their control was ubiquitous in the daily life. It was no longer a matter of a boss's private army governing the life of a town or village but of warlords assuming basic state functions such as taxation, security, and justice throughout entire regions. And if these warlords had "patrimonialist" designs on society – that is, the aim to accumulate capital from the violent domination of that society – achieving their goal was dependent on effectively combating the guerrillas. Only by expelling guerrillas could they monopolize the revenues from drug trafficking.

For many sectors of Colombian society, FARC's offensive in the mid-1990s helped legitimize the new paramilitarism brought about by the Castaño brothers. With the resources, troops, and territory that FARC had accumulated in the previous decades, the guerrillas' leadership was eager to escalate the war. The stakes were high after they succeeded in splitting their units to make continued forays into new regions and multiplying the guerrilla troops: FARC was facing off against the Colombian army in open combat (Rangel 1998; Henderson 2012). The string of military defeats suffered by the army at the hands of FARC between 1996 and 1998 led to a sense of anxiety in the big cities, whose residents feared that the fighting could eventually reach their streets. The military achievements of this guerrilla organization led Pastrana's government (1998–2002) to concede a demilitarized zone in the municipality of El

---

[51] See, for instance, the report by Human Rights Watch: https://bit.ly/3RFR4is.

Cagüán, Caquetá, an area larger than Switzerland, in order to advance a peace process in the middle of the conflict. In that zone, FARC was allowed to become the recognized authority, whereas in the rest of the country the war continued. Even though from 1999 onward the army had demonstrated clear superiority in open combat, for the population of peripheral areas and, in general, most locations outside of the major cities, the situation remained drastic. The incidence kidnapping and extortion reached such onerous and chaotic levels that in many regions the inhabitants welcomed the oligopolies and monopolies of coercion imposed by the Castaño brothers' warlord armies.[52]

Initially, the Castaño brothers limited their ambitions to the department of Cordoba and the region of Urabá. But before long their expansion had rapidly spread into other parts of Colombia. They conquered the rest of the northern coast and the Magdalena Medio before turning to the Llanos Orientales, Caquetá, Putumayo, and even the Pacific coast. Only the most organized paramilitaries with strong social roots – such as the self-defense forces of the Sierra Nevada, those of Ramon Isaza, and those of Carranza in the Llanos – could survive the arrival of the Castaño armies (Duncan 2006). Often in the wake of bloodshed, they would agree to new territorial divisions. In 1997 the Castaño brothers named their initiative the AUC. Though clearly under the leadership of Carlos and Vicente Castaño, the AUC was actually a confederation of regional warlords that gained autonomy as it accumulated strength. By the late 1990s, the control of drug trafficking in Colombia was divided between the AUC and the Norte del Valle Cartel. While the latter only controlled a specific region within the country with private armies of hitmen, they managed a great many of the international routes. In the meantime, they had to pay a significant portion of their earnings to the AUC's warlords, who controlled the coca crops, cocaine laboratories, and transport corridors.

In fact, the power obtained by the warlords of the AUC over the main corridors and centers of drug production meant that the control of drug profits moved from the big-city cartels to the warlords of the countryside. More surpluses from drugs were feeding and increasing peripheral markets. Since the 1980s, cocaine money had been reaching the periphery, but now the armed organizations there, instead of the cartels of Medellín and Cali, were in charge of Colombian drug trafficking. At first, the new situation seemed more problematic for the state: In the periphery, the capacity of these private armies to challenge state authority was greater. The oligopolies and monopolies of

---

[52] In several interviews with paramilitaries and people living in the places where they operated, I was informed that sometimes the initiative to enter a region was the result of a request that they do so by local entrepreneurs, landowners, politicians, and ordinary people who were fed up with the guerrillas' abuses.

coercion imposed by AUC warlords were a symptom of the flaws in the state's monopoly of force in the territory. However, the new situation also meant a significant gain for the state: the control of drug trafficking was displaced toward the periphery, and with this change the state actually recovered a lot of power.

Another expression of the AUC's expansion was the intensification of the role of regional politicians as mediators with the central state. The AUC armies' achievements in terms of social domination quickly translated into advantages in electoral competition. They were able to marshal abundant resources and coercive capacity to define the electoral results in many towns, small and middle-sized cities, and even departments. In 2004 their role in politics was so evident that the scandal finally broke. Innumerable politicians, across entire regions of Colombia, were accused of having links with the AUC. In the end, hundreds of politicians went to prison. The trials and the media reports of the "Parapolitics"[53] scandal demonstrated the role of the political class as mediators in the order imposed by the AUC, as well as how the spread of Parapolitics was capable of transforming the electoral map of Colombia. And, in contrast with the *Proceso 8000*, it was the massive use of coercion, not just the prevalence of drug money, that reshaped the electoral results throughout entire regions (Lopez 2007, 2010; Duncan 2018).

Yet, it was not all strawberries and cream in the relationships between politicians and warlords. While it is true that many members of the political class found an advantage in the countless votes won for them by force, very soon politicians realized that the growing power of the AUC warlords was progressively displacing them. Some congressmen were forced to cede their seats in congress to politicians with closer ties to some AUC warlord. In the subnational governments, elected mayors and governors had no choice but to negotiate with warlords when it came to important appointments in local government and in deciding a large share of the public budget. The case of Mancuso and Lopez Cabrales in the region of Córdoba during the late 1990s illustrates this tension. In order to enter the city of Montería, the Castaño brothers allied themselves with a paramilitary leader from the local elite, Salvatore Mancuso. Although they managed to increase their power and turn the region into the epicenter of Colombia's paramilitary counterinsurgency, the region's largest political clan, the Lopez Cabrales family, retained an electoral majority in spite of its rivalry with Mancuso. So powerful in elections were the Lopez Cabrales candidates that the political class backed by Mancuso had to

---

[53] Despite the transformation of paramilitaries into warlords during the leadership of Castaño, the media still referred to them as paramilitaries.

negotiate with them over the management of local government. For this very reason, the political head of the family, Juan Manuel Lopez Cabrales, was subsequently imprisoned. Ironically, Mancuso not only led the resistance against the guerrillas and Lopez Cabrales' political dominance; he also spearheaded efforts to prevent drug traffickers and paramilitaries from other regions from entering the city. As a relative of the Lopez Cabrales family told me in a personal interview: "It is true that Mancuso caused us a great deal of harm and led to the unjust imprisonment of our relatives. But if it were not for Mancuso, the Países [people from the region of Antioquia] would have devastated Montería."[54]

In the long run, the expansion of the AUC's oligopolies of coercion reached a point at which the central state began to eye them with apprehension. Though the Castaño brothers were initially able to control their troops' expansion, their vast military diffusion throughout the country eventually led to an inevitable fragmentation into different factions. Both brothers wound up being killed by other warlords. It should not come as a surprise to learn that as soon as the FARC had been contained during Uribe's government (2002–10), the very same political establishment that had links with paramilitarism began putting limits on the AUC's aspirations for power. This resulted in its demobilization through a peace process in 2006, but it would not be the end of the warlords. As soon as the AUC demobilized, new private armies sprang up to take its place, replacing it in many peripheral zones. However, they were never even close to reaching the power of the former AUC, nor was the scope of the appropriation of state functions by these new criminal organizations anywhere near commensurable. Furthermore, in personal interviews, former AUC warlords admitted to me that just before signing the peace agreement in 2004, it had been almost impossible to control the middle-ranking commanders, who had revolted and created their own private armies in strategic regions for the production and transportation of cocaine. They were smaller versions of the AUC's previous oligopolies and monopolies of coercion.

The Expansion of the State

After more than three decades of wars, the Colombian state has done an impressive job of expanding its institutions. In the early 1980s it was not even powerful enough to prevent a drug trafficker from the country's second-largest city from declaring war on the state. In peripheral areas the situation was even worse. Irregular armed groups, including guerrillas, paramilitaries and, later, warlords, operated with near-total impunity. Thus, the state had to work hard on

---

[54] Interview in Monteria. June 2008. The name of the interviewee has been kept anonymous.

strengthening its institutions and expanding their presence deep into the periphery. The war was not going to be won by military superiority alone. Had that been the case, it would have had little trouble, since its coercive capacity had always been superior. Rather, its problem lay in extending its ability to rule societies that were under the control of the institutions of cartels, paramilitaries, warlords, and guerrillas. In other words, the state, despite enjoying clear military superiority, did not govern the people in the marginal and peripheral areas of society that had previously been of no interest for the state but could now pose a challenge as a result of drug trafficking.

Today the Colombian state still needs to assert its control over many parts of the country ruled by armed groups. However, the situation has evolved for the better, and state institutions have been gradually catching up. The reduction in the drug traffickers' ability to maintain social control through their coercive apparatuses has been notable – so much so that in some cases they have been reduced to controlling purely criminal affairs. Medellín is a good example of this transformation. After the death of Escobar, Don Berna, a leader of "Los Pepes," assumed the role of mafia boss. In a way, his triumph was a replica of Escobar's approach: Medellín's drug traffickers were to pay a portion of their revenues in exchange for protection. With these resources, Don Berna had almost all of the bandits and the gangs of the city on his payroll. However, unlike Escobar, Don Berna did not challenge the state but instead worked closely with it. In exchange for bribes and bringing order to the criminal underworld, Don Berna got to monopolize the protection racket for illegal businesses. His dominance lasted until he was extradited to the United States in 2008. After that, the mafia in Medellín weakened, no longer controlling international drug-trafficking routes. Private armies in the countryside were now in control of the exportation of cocaine. The Medellín mafia limited its business to local activities such as drug retailing, racketeering, and shark-loan and debt collection, which were to some extent subject to the approval of corrupt police members. One of Pablo Escobar's former hitmen, who controlled one of Medellín's neighborhoods, informed me that during the time of Escobar none of them were thinking about monopolizing the retail sales of drugs in a similar way to the current leaders of city gangs. Then, their main income came from contracts with and salaries from international drug traffickers. Thus, although gangs and organized crime still maintain an extraordinary level of control in many neighborhoods, acting as a parallel state, their economic power has dramatically fallen.

The expansion of the state's regulatory capacity[55] has not only occurred in places where drug trafficking led to the emergence of private armies.

---

[55] For a rigorous estimation of state capacity before and after the conflict see Giraldo et al. (2019).

The guerrillas' military advances in the mid-1990s brought about a strong reaction from the state, which dramatically increased its coercive capacity: the army went from 132,554 to 298,573 soldiers between 2000 and 2009,[56] and security spending went from 2.4 percent of GDP during the Gaviria administration (1990–4) to 4.2 percent during Alvaro Uribe's first term (2002–6) (Lopez 2010). In 2002, under Uribe's government, the state began an offensive to defeat the guerrillas. In the initial phase, the guerrillas were forced to withdraw into the remotest parts of the periphery. Subsequently, aerial bombing campaigns began to kill important leaders. Finally, in 2011, FARC's leader Alfonso Cano was killed in a special operation. Because of its precarious military situation, FARC signed a peace agreement in 2016. Since then, there has been no armed organization with real intentions of replacing the central state.

From the point of view of the Colombian state, the new situation is a marked improvement over the way things were only a decade ago. Although armed groups still exist – from mafias and gangs in the cities to warlords and ELN[57] and FARC dissidents in rural areas – the control they exert over the population has been restricted to the extent that it only affects the most isolated and marginal societies. An uncontestable proof of the outstanding advances of the Colombian state is that even though coca fields are more numerous and cocaine production higher than ever, the oligopolies and monopolies of coercion have experienced a dramatic retreat to even more peripheral zones; there are more coca plantations – more market inclusion in the periphery – but there is less social control by private armies. Furthermore, at present, it no longer seems that the political class in those regions has to rely on the resources and coercive support of criminal organizations to be competitive in elections for a place in the congress, the governorship of a department, or the mayoralty of an important city.

6 Conclusions

The patterns of configuration of oligopolies and monopolies of coercion in Colombia followed the logic proposed here: Ruling institutions run by drug-trafficking organizations usually arose in the peripheral areas where flaws in the state's institutions limited its ability to project its authority. However, in the long term, the trajectories of these patterns led to a process of expansion of the

---

[56] See the official document of the Ministry of Defense "Política de defensa y seguridad todos por un nuevo país," February 2016. Available at: https://bit.ly/3z8PnCI.

[57] The ELN still exists, but in an interview with a former member, I was informed that this guerilla group's military front is not aiming for revolution, but to maintain territorial control. Its commanders act more like warlords than revolutionaries.

coercive capacity of the state toward the periphery. A reconfiguration of the state took place, in which its institutions advanced in the regulation of societies that had been previously governed for the most part by the institutions put in place by the irregular armies who were in control of drug trafficking. But this is a peculiarity of the Colombian trajectory. In other cases, the state's reaction did not necessarily lead to a strengthening of a central authority. In Mexico, for example, politicians at the subnational level controlled the local drug traffickers during the hegemony of the Partido Revolucionario Institucional (PRI) When the democratization process began in the late 1990s, these politicians lost the resources and support of the central state (Astorga 2005; Flores 2013). As a result, the cartels imposed their oligopolies and monopolies of coercion in many regions of Mexico. As of today, despite the war against the cartels, the central state has not been able to recover its coercive capacity. Cartels colluded with corrupted politicians to determine who ruled in the periphery and under what institutions. The particular interactions between drug traffickers and political authorities led to a different trajectory of state configuration in Mexico (Trejos and Ley 2020).

But beyond the particularities of each case, seeing drug trafficking as part of the state configuration trajectories of some countries has three important implications. First, the war on drugs in the countries that supply drugs to the world market invokes something far more complex than the suppression of supply for final consumers. It involves a conflict both between the state and criminal organizations as well as between and within criminal organizations concerning their ability to rule large sectors of society. Whereas security and law enforcement agencies in the United States (such as the United States Drug Enforcement Administration, or DEA) perceive this as a problem linked to criminality with effects on larger security issues, for states like Colombia the problem is mainly political: that of how to deal with criminal organizations that, in addition to controlling drug production and traffic, assume state functions.

The second implication is derived from the first. Where the main goal of certain criminal organizations is to establish rule over a population, then clashes between the groups and the state are likely to result in excessive violence against civilians.[58] Violence against civilians serves as a fundamental means of territorial control. Any civilian suspected of supplying information to a rival may be murdered. Even worse, in the context of these irregular wars the systemic murder of civilians is a common practice, regardless of actual levels of

---

[58] The logic of violence against civilians in civil wars (Kalyvas 2006) shares a lot of similarities with these wars.

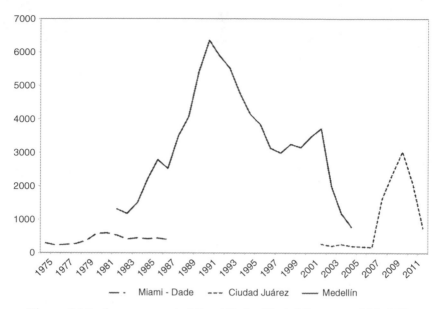

Figure 2 Murders per year in Miami Dade, Ciudad Juarez, and Medellín
Data sources: For Miami Dade, Stauffer (2001); for Ciudad Juarez, Alarcon (2014); and for Medellín, Giraldo (2008).

collaboration. A simple comparison between three cities with similar numbers of inhabitants shows the difference in levels of violence against civilians that reflect where drug traffickers are competing to govern society (see Figure 2). In Miami Dade, due to a bloody vendetta between Colombian traffickers during the 1980s, murders jumped from 227 murders per year in the mid-1970s to 602 in 1981. Despite the number of murders almost tripling, Miami Dade's figures seem low when compared to Medellín during the time of Escobar, when figures ballooned from a few more than 1,000 murders in 1983 to 6,349 in 1991, and Ciudad Juarez, when the Sinaloa cartel sought to expel the local cartel, and the murder rate skyrocketed from 173 murders in 2007 to more than 3,000 three years later. The wars in Medellín and Juarez involved control over civilians.

The third and final implication of this study is that the institutions imposed by criminal organizations, though not necessarily created as part of a broader political project, often do offer solutions to the demands of large sectors of society. The private armies funded by drug lords and the revenues derived from drug trafficking can offer protection, a form of law enforcement, and participation in global consumption, which would otherwise be unavailable to much of society. In order to neutralize monopolies and oligopolies of coercion, states must be able to compete in terms of responding to social demands where its institutions have a clear disadvantage. Ultimately, the political implications of drug trafficking in countries like Colombia revolve around the central question of how power and order are organized in the periphery when a significant part of this periphery has access to world markets through the drug industry and its massive revenues.

References

Aguilera, Mario (2013). "Las FARC: Auge y quiebre del modelo de guerra." *Análisis Político*, January–April, pp. 85–111.

Aguilera, Mario (2014). *Contrapoder y justicia guerrillera: fragmentación política y orden insurgente en Colombia (1952–2003)*. Bogotá: IEPRI.

Alarcon, Cesar (2014). "Ciudad Juárez: Sociedad, criminalidad y violencia trasnacional." In A. M. Jaramillo, *Ciudades en la encrucijada: violencia y poder criminal en Río de Janeiro, Medellín, Bogotá y Ciudad Juárez*, 249. Medellín: Corporación Región.

Andreas, Peter and Ethan Nadelmann (2013). *Policing the Globe: Criminalization and Crime Control in International Relations*. Oxford: Oxford University Press.

Angarita, Pablo, Hector Gallo, and Blanca Jimenez (2008). *Dinámicas de guerra y construcción de paz: Estudio interdisciplinario del conflicto armado en la Comuna 13 de Medellín*. Medellín: University of Antioquia, University of Medellín, IPC Region.

Appadurai, Arjun (1991). "Introducción: las mercancías y la política del valor." In *La vida social de las cosas. Perspectiva cultural de las mercancías*, edited by Arjun Appadurai, 13–17. Cambridge: Cambridge University Press Editorial; Mexico City: Grijalbo.

Arango Jaramillo, Mario (1988). *Impacto del narcotráfico en Antioquia*. Medellín: Editorial J. M. Arango.

Arias, Desmond (2017). *Criminal Enterprises and Governance in Latin America and the Caribbean*. Cambridge: Cambridge University Press.

Arjona, Ana (2017). *Rebelocracy: Social Order in the Colombian Civil War*. Cambridge: Cambridge University Press.

Astorga, Luis (1995). *Mitologia del narcotraficante en Mexico*. Mexico City: Plaza y Janés.

(2005). *El siglo de las drogas*. Mexico City: Plaza & Janes.

Auyero, Javier (2007). *Routine Politics and Violence in Argentina: The Gray Zone of State Power*. New York: Cambridge University Press.

Baquero, Petrite (2012). *El ABC de la mafia*. Bogotá: Planeta.

Barnes, Nicholas (2017). "Criminal Politics: An Integrated Approach to the Study of Organized Crime, Politics, and Violence." *Perspectives on Politics* 15, no. 4 (December): 967–87.

Bernal, Fernando (2004). *Crisis algodonera y violencia en el departamento del Cesar*. Bogotá: Cuadernos PNUD–MPS.

Betancourt, Dario (1998). *Mediadores, rebuscadores, traquetos y narcos: Valle del Cauca 1890–1997*. Bogotá: Ediciones Antropos.

Boone, Catherine (2003). *Political Topographies of the African State*. Cambridge: Cambridge University Press.

Camacho, Alvaro (2010). "Mafia: los usos de un concepto polisémico y su aplicabilidad al caso colombiano. (a propósito del libro de Diego Gambetta)." *Historia Crítica* 41 (May/August).

Centeno, Miguel (2003). *Blood and Debt: War and the Nation-State in Latin America*. University Park, PA: Penn State University Press.

Chepesiuk, Ron (2005). *Drug Lords: The Rise and Fall of the Cali Cartel*. Preston: Milo Books.

Civico, Aldo (2010). *No divulgar hasta que los implicados estén muertos: las guerras de "Doblecero."* Bogotá: Intermedio Editores.

Claver Tellez, Pedro (1993). *La guerra verde: Treinta años de conflicto entre los esmeralderos*. Bogotá: Intermedio Editores.

Dewey, Matías (2015). *El orden clandestino: politica, fuerzas de seguridad y mercados ilegales en la Argentina*. Buenos Aires: Katz Editores.

Douglas, Mary, and Baron Isherwood (1981). *The World of Goods*. London: Routledge.

Dudley, Steven (2008). *Armas y urnas: Historia de un genocidio politico*. Bogotá: Planeta.

Duffield, Mark (1998). "Post-Modern Conflict: Warlords, Post-Adjustment States and Private Protection." *Civil Wars* 1, no. 1: 65-102.

Duncan, Gustavo (2006). *Los señores de la guerra*. Bogotá: Editorial Planeta.

(2013). "Una lectura politica de Pablo Escobar." *Co-Herencia* 10, no. 19: 235–62.

(2018). *Democracia feroz*. Bogotá: Debate.

Duran, Angelica (2017). *The Politics of Drug Violence: Criminals, Cops and Politicians in Colombia and Mexico*. Oxford: Oxford University Press.

Eaton, Kent (2006). "The Downside of Decentralisation: Armed Clientelism in Colombia." *Security Studies* 15: 533–62.

Echandia, Camilo (2006). *Dos decadas de escalamiento del conflicto armado en Colombia (1986–2006)*. Bogotá: Editorial Universidad Externado de Colombia.

Edberg, Mark (2004). *El Narcotraficante: Narcocorridos and the Construction of a Cultural Persona on the US–Mexican Border*. Austin: University of Texas Press.

Elias, Norbert (1994). *The Civilizing Process*. Oxford: Blackwell.

Fajardo, Dario (2002). *Para sembrar la paz, hay que aflojar la tierra: Comunidades, tierras y territorios en la construccion de un pais.* Bogotá: Universidad Nacional de Colombia.

Flores, Carlos (2013). *Historia de polvo y sangre: génesis y evolución del tráfico de drogas en el estado de Tamaulipas.* Mexico City: CIESAS.

Gaitan, Fernando (1995). "Una indagacion sobre las causas de la violencia." In *Dos ensayos especulativos sobre la violencia en Colombia*, edited by M. Deas and F. Gaitán Daza, 13–99. Bogotá: Fonade.

Gallant, Thomas (1999). "Brigandage, Piracy, Capitalism, and State-Formation: Transnational Crime from a Historical World-Systems Perspective." In *States and Illegal Practices*, edited by Josiah Heyman, 25–61. London: Berg.

Gambetta, Diego (2007). *La mafia siciliana: El negocio de la proteccion privada.* Mexico City: Fondo de Cultura Economica.

Garcia Villegas, Mauricio, and Espinosa Restrepo, Jose Rafael (2012). "Crimen, conflicto armado y Estado en Colombia, México y Guatemala." Bogotá: Documentos de discusión, DEJUSTICIA.

Gibson, Edward (2004). "Subnational Authoritarianism: Territorial Strategies of Political Control in Democratic Regimes." Paper prepared for delivery at the 2004 Annual Meeting of the American Political Science Association, Washington, DC.

Giraldo, Jorge (2008). *Seguridad en Medellín: El exito, sus explicaciones, limitaciones y fragilidades.* Washington, DC: Wilson Center.

(2015). *Las ideas en la Guerra.* Bogotá: Editorial Debate.

Giraldo, Jorge, Jose Fortou, and Maria Gomez (2019). "200 años de guerra y paz en Colombia: numeros y rasgos estilizados." *Co-Herencia* 16, no.31: 357–71.

Giraudy, Agustina, Eduardo Moncada, and Richard Snyder (eds.) (2019). *Inside Countries: Subnational Research in Comparative Politics.* Cambridge: Cambridge University Press.

Gonzalez, Fernan (2003). "Colapso parcial o presencia diferenciada del estado en Colombia? Una mirada desde la historia?" *Colombia Internacional* 58: 124–58.

(2014). *Poder y violencia en Colombia.* Bogotá: Odecofi, Cinep.

Gonzalez, Fernan, Ingrid Bolivar, and Teofilo y Vazquez (2003). *Violencia politica en Colombia: De la nacion fragmentada a la construccion del Estado.* Bogotá: Cinep.

Gootenberg, Paul (2008). *Andean Cocaine: The Making of a Global Drug.* Chapel Hill: University of North Carolina Press.

Gouëset, Vincent (1998). *Bogota, nacimiento de una metropoli: La originali-dad del proceso de concentración urbana en Colombia en el siglo XX.* Bogotá: Tercer Mundo Editores.

Gutierrez Sanin, Francisco (2019). *Clientelistic Warfare: Paramilitaries and the State in Colombia (1982–2007).* Oxford: Peter Lang.

Henderson, James (2006). *La modernizacion en Colombia: Los años de Laureano Gomez, 1889–1965.* Medellín: University of Antioquia.

(2012). *Víctima de la globalización. La historia de como el narcotráfico destruyo la paz en Colombia.* Bogotá: Siglo del Hombre Editores.

Hincapie, Edilberto and Leonardo Correa (2005). "Testimonio del comercio en Guayaquil." Doctoral thesis, University of Medellín.

Jansson, Oscar (2008). *The Cursed Leaf: An Anthropology of the Political Economy of Cocaine Production in Southern Colombia.* Uppsala: Uppsala University.

Jaramillo, Jaíme, Leónidas Mora, and Fernando Cubides (1989). *Colonizacion, coca y guerrilla,* 3rd ed. Bogotá: Alianza Editorial Colombiana.

Kalyvas, Stathis (2006). *The Logic of Violence in Civil War.* Cambridge: Cambridge University Press.

Kenney, Michael C. (2007). *From Pablo to Osama: Trafficking and Terrorist Networks, Government Bureaucracies, and Competitive Adaptation.* University Park, PA: Penn State University Press.

Krauthausen, Ciro (1998). *Padrinos y mercaderes, crimen organizado en Italia y Colombia.* Bogotá: Editorial Espasa.

Leal, Francisco, and Andres Davila (1990). *Clientelismo: El sistema politico y su expresion regional.* Bogotá: Instituto de Estudios Politicos y Relaciones Internacionales (IEPRI).

Lee, Martyn J. (1993) *Consumer Culture Reborn: The Cultural Politics of Consumption.* London: Routledge.

Legarda, Astrid (2005). *El verdadero Pablo: Sangre, traicion y muerte … En las confesiones de Alias "Popeye" su principal lugarteniente.* Bogotá: Ediciones Dipon.

Lemaitre, Julieta (2011). *La paz en cuestion: La guerra y la paz en la Asamblea Constituyente de 1991.* Bogotá: Ediciones Uniandes.

Lessing, Benjamin (2017). *Making Peace in Drug Wars: Crackdowns and Cartels in Latin America.* Cambridge: Cambridge University Press.

(2020). *Conceptualizing Criminal Governance.* Cambridge: Cambridge University Press.

Londoño, Oscar (1989). *Colonizacion del Ariari, 1950–1970: Aproximacion a una historia regional.* Villavicencio: Centro de Estudios Sociales para el Desarrollo de los Llanos.

Lopez, Claudia (2007). *La parapolitica*. Bogotá: Intermedio Editores.

(2010). *Y refundaron la patria*. Bogotá: Debate.

(2016). *Adios a las Farc. ¿y ahora que?* Bogotá: Debate.

Mann, Michael (1984). *The Autonomous Power of the State: Its Origins, Mechanisms, and Results*. In *States in History*, edited by John A. Hall, 185–213. Oxford: Blackwell.

(1986). *The Sources of Social Power*. Cambridge University Press.

Martin, Gerard (2012). *Medellín tragedia y resurrección: Mafia, ciudad y estado: 1975–2012*. Bogotá: Editorial Planeta.

Medina Gallego, Carlos (1990). *Autodefensas, paramilitares y narcotráfico en Colombia: Origen, desarrollo y consolidación: El caso "Puerto Boyacá."* Bogotá: Editorial Documentos Periodísticos.

Mejia, Daniel, and Daniel Rico (2011). "La microeconomía de la producción y tráfico de cocaína en Colombia." In *Políticas antidrogas en Colombia: Éxitos, fracasos y extravíos*, edited by Alejandro Gaviria, and Daniel Mejia, 15–40. Bogotá: Universidad de los Andes.

Migdal, Joel (1988). *Strong Societies and Weak States: State–Society Relations and State Capabilities in the Third World*. Princeton, NJ: Princeton University Press.

Misse, Michel (2007). "Illegal Markets, Protection Rackets and Organized Crime in Rio de Janeiro." *Estudos Avançados* 21, no. 61: 139–57.

Moncada, Eduardo (2013). "The Politics of Urban Violence: Challenges for Development in the Global South." *Studies in Comparative International Development* 48, no. 3: 217–39.

Molano, Alfredo (1987). *Selva adentro: Una historia oral sobre la colonizacion del Guaviare*. Bogotá: Ancora Editores.

Moore, Barrington (1978). *Injustice: The Social Bases of Obedience and Revolt*. New York: M. E. Sharpe.

O'Donnell, Guillermo (1993). "On the State, Democratization and Some Conceptual Problems: A Latin American View with Glances at Some Postcommunist Countries." *World Development* 21, no. 8: 1355–69.

Olson, Mancur (1993). "Dictatorship, Democracy, and Development." *American Political Science Review* 87, no. 3: 567–76.

Pizarro, Eduardo (1991). *Las FARC (1949–1966): De la autodefensa a la combinacion de todas las formas de lucha*. Bogotá: UN, Instituto de Estudios Politicos y Relaciones Internacionales (IEPRI).

(2002). "La atomizacion partidista en Colombia: el fenomeno de las micro-empresas electorales." In *Degradación o cambio: Evolución del sistema político colombiano*, edited by Francisco Gutiérrez, 359–401. Bogotá: IEPRI/Norma.

Pizarro, Eduardo and Maria Bejarano (2003). "Colombia: A Failed State?" *Revista: Harvard Review of Latin America* 2, no. 3 (2003): 1–6.

Ramsey, William (1981). *Guerrilleros y soldados*. Bogotá: Tercer Mundo.

Rangel, Alfredo (1998). *Colombia: Guerra de fin de siglo*. Bogotá: Tercer Mundo Editores.

Rempel, William (2012). *En la boca del lobo: La historia jamas contada del hombre que hizo caer al cartel de Cali*. New York: Vintage.

Reno, William (2002). "Mafia Troubles, Warlord Crises." In *Beyond State Crisis? Postcolonial Africa and Post-Soviet Eurasia in Comparative Perspective*, edited by M. Beissinger and C. Young, 105–29. Baltimore, MD: Johns Hopkins University Press.

Reyes, Alejandro (2009). *Guerreros y campesinos: El despojo de la tierra en Colombia*. Bogotá: Editorial Norma.

Romero, Mauricio (2003). *Paramilitares y autodefensas, 1982–2003*. Bogotá: Instituto de Estudios Politicos y Relaciones Internacionales (IEPRI).

Ronderos, Maria Teresa (2014). *Guerras recicladas*. Bogotá: Debate.

Salazar, Alonso (2001). *La parabola de Pablo*. Bogotá: Editorial Planeta.

Sanchez, Fabio, and Mario Chacon (2005). "Conflicto, Estado y descentralizacion: Del progreso social a la disputa armada por el control local, 1974–2002." Working Paper Series 1, Documento de Trabajo No. 70, Crisis States Programme, Bogotá.

Sanchez, Toño, Jr. (2010). *Cronicas que da miedo contar*. Montería: Codice Producciones Limitada.

Sassen, Saskia (2002). *The Global City*. Princeton, NJ: Princeton University Press.

Scott, James (2000). *Los dominados y el arte de la resistencia: Discursos ocultos*. Mexico: Ediciones Era.

Shils, Edward. (1974). Centre and Periphery: Essays in Macrosociology (Selected Papers of Edward Shils, 2). Chicago: University of Chicago Press.

Skaperdas, Stergios (1995). "The Political Economy of Organized Crime: Providing Protection When the State Does Not." *Economics of Governance* 2: 173–202.

Skaperdas, Stergios, and Constantinos Syropoulos (1995). "Gangs as Primitive States." In *The Economics of Organized Crime*, edited by G. Fiorentini and S. Peltzman, 61–81. Cambridge: Cambridge University Press.

Soifer, Hillel David (2015). *State Building in Latin America*. Cambridge: Cambridge University Press.

Stauffer, Eric (2001). *Homicides in Miami Dade County, Florida*. Miami: Scholarly Forum, Florida International University.

Thoumi, Francisco (1994). *Economia politica y narcotrafico*. Bogotá: Tercer Mundo Editores.

Tilly, Charles (1985). "War Making and State Making as Organized Crime." In *Bringing the State Back In*, edited by Peter Evans, Dietrich Rueschemeyer, and Theda Skocpol, 169–91. New York: Cambridge.

(2001). *Coercion, Capital and European States: AD 990–1992*. Cambridge, MA: John Wiley & Sons.

Tobon, Santiago (2012). "Do Institutions Affect the Expansion of Illicit Crops?" (Master's thesis in Economic Sciences, Economics School of Louvain).

Torres, Maria Clara (2012). "Coca, politica y Estado: El caso de Putumayo, 1978–2006." (Master's thesis in Political Studies and International Relations, Universidad Nacional de Colombia)

Trejos, Guillermo and Sandra Ley (2020). *Votes, Drugs, and Violence: The Political Logic of Criminal Wars in Mexico*. Cambridge: Cambridge University Press.

Uribe Alarcon, Maria Victoria (1992). *Limpiar la tierra: Guerra y poder entre esmeralderos*. Bogotá: CINEP.

Vanegas, Martin, Gustavo Duncan, and Santiago Tobon (2021). *Más allá de la codicia y el agravio: El caso de la formación de mercados en la periferia colombiana*. Medellín: Ediciones Universidad EAFIT.

Varese, Federico (2001). *The Russian Mafia: Private Protection in a New Market Economy*. Oxford: Oxford University Press.

(2017). *Mafia Life: Love, Death and Money at the Heart of Organised Crime*. London: Profile Books.

Vargas, Mauricio, Jorge Lesmes, and Edgar Tellez (1996). *El presidente que se iba a caer: Diario secreto de tres periodistas sobre el 8000*. Bogotá: Planeta Colombiana Editorial S. A.

Velazquez, Jorge E. (1992). *Como me infiltre y engañe al cartel*. Bogotá: Editorial Oveja Negra.

Volkov, Vadim (2002). *Violent Entrepreneurs: The Use of Force in the Making of Russian Capitalism*. New York: Cornell University Press.

Weber, Max (1944). *Economia y sociedad*. Mexico DF: Fondo De Cultura Económica.

Wickham-Crowley, Timothy (1992). *Guerrillas and Revolution in Latin America: A Comparative Study of Insurgents and Regimes since 1956*. Princeton, NJ: Princeton University Press.

Acknowledgments

To my sons, Santiago and Antonio . . . to my friend Gustavo . . . and to Ana.

I am grateful to Andreas Feldman, Jorge Giraldo, Francisco Thoumi, Álvaro Camacho and Juan Pablo Luna. Without their support it would not have been possible to write this book.

Cambridge Elements⁼

Politics and Society in Latin America

Maria Victoria Murillo

Columbia University

Maria Victoria Murillo is Professor of Political Science and International Affairs at Columbia University. She is the author of *Political Competition, Partisanship, and Policymaking in the Reform of Latin American Public Utilities* (Cambridge, 2009). She is also editor of *Carreras Magisteriales, Desempeño Educativo y Sindicatos de Maestros en América Latina* (2003), and co-editor of *Argentine Democracy: the Politics of Institutional Weakness* (2005). She has published in edited volumes as well as in the *American Journal of Political Science, World Politics*, and *Comparative Political Studies*, among others.

Tulia G. Falleti

University of Pennsylvania

Tulia G. Falleti is the Class of 1965 Endowed Term Professor of Political Science, Director of the Latin American and Latino Studies Program, and Senior Fellow of the Leonard Davis Institute for Health Economics at the University of Pennsylvania. She received her BA in Sociology from the Universidad de Buenos Aires and her Ph.D. in Political Science from Northwestern University. Falleti is the author of *Decentralization and Subnational Politics in Latin America* (Cambridge University Press, 2010), which earned the Donna Lee Van Cott Award for best book on political institutions from the Latin American Studies Association, and with Santiago Cunial of *Participation in Social Policy: Public Health in Comparative Perspective* (Cambridge University Press, 2018). She is co-editor, with Orfeo Fioretos and Adam Sheingate, of *The Oxford Handbook of Historical Institutionalism* (Oxford University Press, 2016), among other edited books. Her articles on decentralization, federalism, authoritarianism, and qualitative methods have appeared in edited volumes and journals such as the *American Political Science Review, Comparative Political Studies, Publius, Studies in Comparative International Development*, and *Qualitative Sociology*, among others.

Juan Pablo Luna

The Pontifical Catholic University of Chile

Juan Pablo Luna is Professor of Political Science at The Pontifical Catholic University of Chile. He received his BA in Applied Social Sciences from the UCUDAL (Uruguay) and his PhD in Political Science from the University of North Carolina at Chapel Hill. He is the author of *Segmented Representation. Political Party Strategies in Unequal Democracies* (Oxford University Press, 2014), and has co-authored *Latin American Party Systems* (Cambridge University Press, 2010). In 2014, along with Cristobal Rovira, he co-edited *The Resilience of the Latin American Right* (Johns Hopkins University). His work on political representation, state capacity, and organized crime has appeared in the following journals: *Comparative Political Studies, Revista de Ciencia Política*, the *Journal of Latin American Studies, Latin American Politics and Society, Studies in Comparative International Development, Política y Gobierno, Democratization, Perfiles Latinoamericanos*, and the *Journal of Democracy*.

Andrew Schrank

Brown University

Andrew Schrank is the Olive C. Watson Professor of Sociology and International & Public Affairs at Brown University. He received his BA from the University of Michigan and his PhD from the University of Wisconsin. His articles on business, labor, and the state in Latin America have appeared in the *American Journal of Sociology, Comparative Politics*,

Comparative Political Studies, Latin American Politics & Society, Social Forces,
and *World Development,* among other journals, and his co-authored book, *Root-Cause
Regulation: Labor Inspection in Europe and the Americas,* is forthcoming
at Harvard University Press.

Advisory Board

About the Series

Latin American politics and society are at a crossroads, simultaneously confronting
serious challenges and remarkable opportunities that are likely to be shaped by formal
institutions and informal practices alike. The Elements series on Politics and Society in
Latin America offers multidisciplinary and methodologically pluralist contributions on
the most important topics and problems confronted by the region.

Cambridge Elements ☰

Politics and Society in Latin America

Elements in the Series

A full series listing is available at: www.cambridge.org/PSLT

Printed in the United States
by Baker & Taylor Publisher Services